THE LEGEND OF
BURATAI

VOLUME 2

Lt. General (Dr) T.Y Buratai

with Dr. Abubakar MS

Mereo Books

Mereo Books 2nd Floor, 6-8 Dyer Street,
Cirencester, Gloucestershire, GL7 2PF

An imprint of Memoirs Book Ltd. www.mereobooks.com

First published by:
Sprezzatura Publishing
P.O Box 522, Area 1, Garki, Abuja

http://*www.sprezzaturapublishing.com*
Email:info@*sprezzaturapublishing.com*

First Edition January 2020
Copyright© Lt. General Tukur Yusufu Buratai 2020

A catalogue record for this book is available from the National Library of Nigeria.

ISBN: 978-1-86151-915-3

The facts related in this book are all true. Some names, identities and locations have been changed, in part because of security reasons.

contents

❖ ❖ ❖

ABOUT THIS BOOK

❖ ❖ ❖

The Legend of Buratai Volume II is a comprehensive memoir written by one of Africa's legendary military tacticians and infantry general. The book offers a sublime awareness about the role of destiny and hard work in a man's life while seeking to motivate young people to shun violence, build peace, and strive for excellence. In this book, General Buratai narrates his early life, military career and the relentless war against insurgency. Young people especially cadets, will find his principles of success as outlined in this book very useful.

"I have known and interacted with the principal character of this book right from the 90s at the State House. I have learnt a lot from him and it is good I make it clear that his influence on me contributed in making me a better officer. I am recommending this book to cadets in the NDA and students in other institutions of learning."

Major General Jamil Sarham, Commandant,
Nigerian Defence Academy, Kaduna

The Legend of Buratai Volume II is a fascinating book with a nice mix of military tactics and important life lessons from the mind of one of Nigeria's most notable military strategists. It's an exhilarating read that offers insight into some of the most significant decisions and movements effecting the progression and safety of Nigeria. The Legend of Buratai is a must read for anyone interested in defeating terrorism, military history, and the incredible amount of grit and wisdom it takes to be an effective leader today.

Susan Keillor, LSW, MBA, Freelance Editor and Writer

This second volume of *The Legend of Buratai* is an unbelievable master piece rich in history and aesthetics. When he finally goes to meet his Creator, children who would read this book afterwards would wish they had met General Buratai in person.

This book is capable of reawakening patriotism to our fatherland. I salute the brains behind this Pearl.

Moses A. Uyang, Author and Humanitarian

ABOUT THE AUTHORS

❖ ❖ ❖

Lt. General Buratai is the 20th Chief of Staff of the Nigerian Army in the Chronicles of Command. He graduated from the Nigerian Defence Academy in 1983 as a member of the 29th Regular Course and also gained a degree in History from the University of Maiduguri and a Master's Degree in Philosophy from the University of the Professionals, Bangladesh. In 2018 he was awarded a Doctorate Degree (Honoris Causa) by the Kaduna State University, Kaduna. He is a legendary infantry general who made headlines by defeating the Boko Haram insurgents through his exemplary leadership skills, generalship and bravery. General Buratai is a member of the Military Writers' Society of America (MWSA), International Writers Association (IWA), Association of Nigerian Authors (ANA), and Military Writers' Society of Nigeria.

He served gallantly as Commander of the Multinational Joint Task Force before his appointment as Chief of Army Staff in 2015. He is the recipient of the United Nations Medal for Angolan Verification Medal II, Distinguished Service Star, Meritorious Service Star, Field Command Medal and the Forces Services Star.

General Buratai is not only an infantry general and

a military tactician, he is also a farmer, teacher and a historian par excellence. His hobbies include jogging, golf and farming.

Dr Abubakar holds a Doctorate in Media Leadership as well as Metaphysics and is presently doing postgraduate studies in Terrorism and Political Violence at St. Andrews University. Abubakar has a certificate in Religion, Conflict and Peace from Harvard University and a certificate in Strategic Thinking and Problem Solving from the Metropolitan School of Management and Business, UK. He is a member of the International Auto/Biography Association (IABA), Association of Nigerian Authors (ANA), the Nigerian Union of Journalists (NUJ) and the Nigerian Guild of Editors. He is the co-founder of the Military Writers Society of Nigeria and an active member of the International Writers Association, USA. Abubakar is the author of *The Legend of Buratai Volume One*, *Africa: Reflect, Rethink and Act*, *The Naïve Perspective*, *Dr Dikwa: The Making of an Astute Public Servant* and *The Purple Heart*. He is the Principal partner at Elbroco Security Consultants and a consultant to numerous local NGOs. His hobbies include languages (French and Arabic), walking, meditation, push-ups and chess.

DEDICATIONS

❖ ❖ ❖

This book is dedicated to all young people in Nigeria, and especially those of the Nigerian Military School and the Nigerian Defence Academy. Most of them are looking for role models to emulate; some are searching for inspiration and a few are even confused. It is my hope that this book will give them focus, inspire them and reinvigorate their belief in excellence as a sure path to success.

PUBLISHER'S NOTE

❖ ❖ ❖

Let me start by saying thank you to the Chief of Army Staff, Lt. General T.Y Buratai, who agreed to put down some parts of his life in written form for posterity. Sprezzatura Publishing Ltd considers this a worthy sacrifice from a very busy Nigerian. We appreciate God for giving us the rare opportunity to be the official publisher of this book. His willingness to be actively involved in this project made this volume easier to write because the load was jointly shared. He sacrificed precious time and contributed valuable information that helped tremendously in coming up with this volume. The whole idea behind it was conceived by him. General Buratai is indeed an exemplary officer who not only provided the ideas and inspiration to produce this book but also took his time to read through the manuscript with a fine-toothed comb. He made this book possible through his willingness to put down some of his personal experience in writing for posterity to read.

The recollections of General Buratai's childhood and his formative years in this volume makes this book a more interesting read than the previous volume. With the exception of a few chapters, the entire narration was his. This is why the entire book was written in the first person. We believe that this volume will encourage General Buratai to come up with his autobiography in the near future.

This book has also benefited from the supply of useful

research materials and transcripts of numerous interviews of the COAS by Brigadier Bello Alhaji Tsoho, Provost, Nigerian Army College of Education, Sobi, Ilorin. He gladly provided those documents and also helped with positive suggestions on how to improve the book. He pointed out omissions and gaps in the narrations.

In his preface to *Nigeria's Soldiers of Fortune*, Max Siollun wrote some thought-provoking words about Nigeria. He wrote:

> *Trying to understand Nigeria can be a byzantine experience. It is a place where neighbourhood gossip and rumours are regarded as more reliable purveyors of history and news than books, newspapers and other forms of information. Nigeria's leaders have contributed to this state of affairs... Given its leaders' refusal or reluctance to record their stewardship, or to promote the study of history in schools, Nigeria's history has frequently consisted of urban legends, personal beliefs and rival conspiracy theories that vary depending on the ethnicity, geographic origin or religion of the narrator.*

With this book, General Buratai has made a valuable contribution to our national reservoir of knowledge which will help in the dissemination of accurate information. We believe that young people, especially future cadets, will find this book a treasure.

We are grateful to the staff and management of Sprezzatura Publishing Limited for their efforts and contributions in making this Volume a reality.

Lazarus Samuel Balami

maps

❖ ❖ ❖

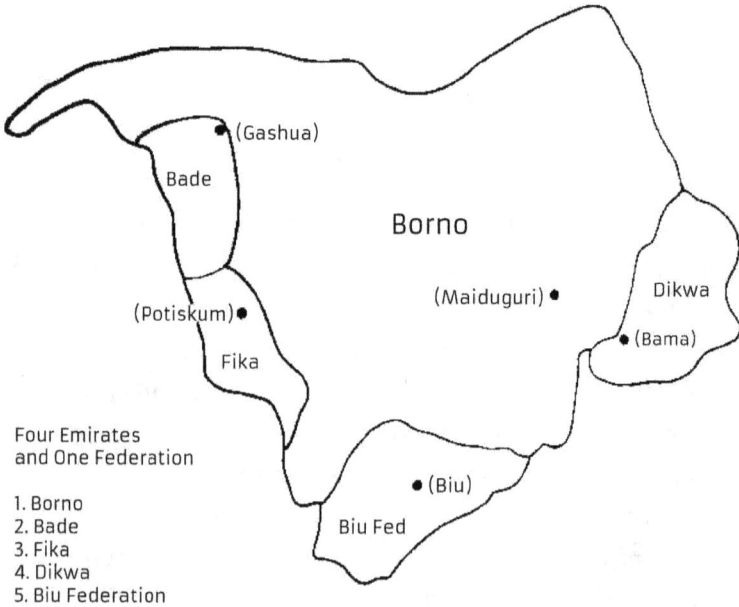

Figure 1.

Map of Borno Province with Native Authority Area

Figure 2.
Map of Biu Emirate

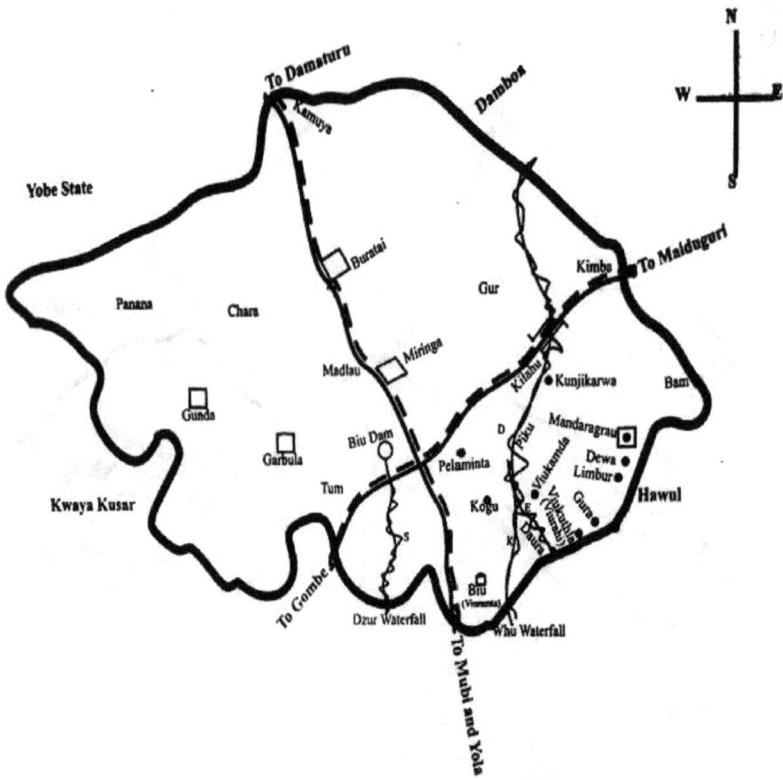

Figure 3.
Map of Biu Local Government Area Showing all former
and present Capitals of the Emirate.

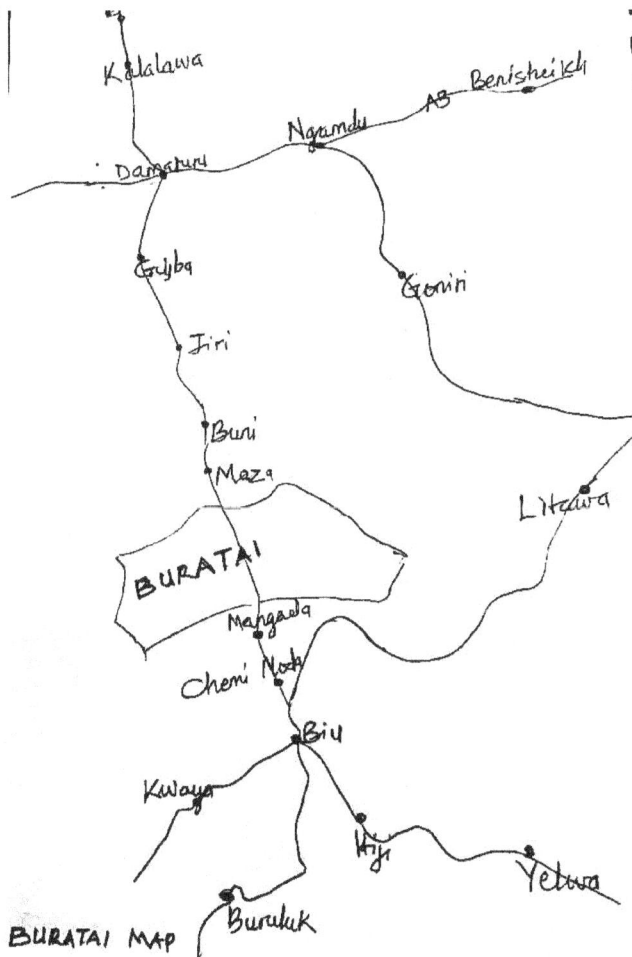

Figure 4.
A rough sketch indicating the location of Buratai.
Its geographical coordinates are 10° 54' 27".

ACKNOWLEDGEMENTS

❖ ❖ ❖

It is pertinent to mention here that Nigeria has come a long way since attaining independence in 1960 and several leaders have left their marks in the sands of time in all spheres of life. It is the contribution of these past leaders that has given us all a platform to become what we are and to also achieve all we have been able to achieve today. Nigeria is still in dire need of leaders of character, charisma and selflessness and with flawless moral character.

It is for this reason that I am hoping that my own modest story will serve as an inspiration and encouragement to our upcoming generation, so that they can aspire to be anything in life. Nigeria is blessed with abundant human and natural resources and opportunities abound everywhere and every time, but it is also important to state that fortune favours the brave. I wish to say once again that I am indeed humbled and encouraged that my relatively obscure story from a humble and simple upbringing, as well as my modest contributions, could serve as a marker to inspire young and aspiring minds in *The Legend of Buratai Volume One*.

I shall forever remain grateful and loyal to President Muhammadu Buhari GCFR, my Commander-in-Chief, for believing in me and appointing me to head one of the strongest and most strategic institutions of Nigeria. I have watched him closely since 1983 when I graduated from the NDA and his discipline and Spartan way of life has served as model for me to emulate. Mr President, you have given me the opportunity to lead a great group of individuals to be a leader of the great Nigerian Army, which is the desire of every officer. Thank you very much, your excellency.

My father would have loved to see this book, but he is no longer with us. I am what I am today because of him. He taught me discipline, tough love, manners, respect, and so much more that has helped me succeed in life. I truly have no idea where I would be if he had not. My profound gratitude also goes to my immediate family members, who displayed resilience and fortitude and stayed together as I carry out my onerous task of leading the Nigerian Army and also squeezing out time to work on this book.

To all the individuals I have had the opportunity to lead, be led by, or watch their leadership from afar, I want to say thank you for being the inspiration and foundation for this book. I must say that without the experiences and support I received from my peers and team at the Nigerian Army, this book would not have existed.

One such boss I served under was Major General I.D. Penap. I learned a lot from him. During the public presentation of the first volume of the book to schoolchildren in Port Harcourt, General Penap said that it is high time the publishers came up with a non-fiction version of the book. He made it clear that this was an important plea that must be complied with.

Writing a book about the story of your life is a surreal process. I'm forever indebted to Dr Abubakar MS and Mr Chris Newton for their editorial help, keen insight, and ongoing support in bringing my stories to life. It is because of their efforts and encouragement that I have a legacy to pass on to my family where none existed before. The efforts of Mr Chris Newton, in detecting facts that were contradictory or didn't really check out, is acknowledged. He, together with Susan Keillor, proofread and helped in editing the draft of this book, which has also benefited from their suggestions for its improvement.

I must also acknowledge with gratitude the support of our publishers, Sprezzatura Publishing Limited and Mereo Books UK, for believing in us and encouraging us to pursue this line of action. They believe that my relatively obscure life is worthy of emulation and went as far as giving us support to produce this second volume of *The Legend of Buratai*. It was the management of Sprezzatura that suggested that the first volume should be written in simple English for school pupils to easily read and understand. They also advised us how to write the second volume and tailor it to suit senior secondary school and tertiary students, especially cadets.

The intellectual support of Dr Bukar Usman, who to my mind is the highest authority on Biu history, is also acknowledged. The good doctor sent me a full carton of books he has authored at no cost. One of the books was his *magnum opus*, *A History of Biu,* and this book provided credible and well-researched information on the history of Biu and its environs, the Babur Bura ethnic nationality and their origin, everything about Buratai, the life and times of Yamtarawala and the Biu Dynasty of today. This Officer of the Order of the Niger is a scholar and author of international repute and his contributions to the development of knowledge to Biu and Nigeria through the Biu Emirate Studies Series is still under-appreciated by the

Borno State Government. As far as this book is concerned, I shall remain indebted to Dr Usman, and for this I say thank you, sir.

I shall always remain faithful, loyal and honest to my Fatherland. I trust you to do the same.

Lieutenant General Tukur Yusuf Buratai

November 2019

FOREWORD

❖ ❖ ❖

It is my singular honour to be called upon to write the foreword of the memoir of General Tukur Buratai, BA (Hons) MA MPhil PhD Chief of Staff the Nigerian Army.

General Buratai's record of service as Chief of Staff of the Nigerian Army is legendary and cannot be surpassed. He is a General who inspires his subjects by leading from the front. Cool and calculated, I can say General Buratai has set a record of bravery against a stubborn enemy whose ideology is difficult to change but despite that, General Buratai continues to record successes through authentic leadership. As someone who has read this book before others, I can say with all sense of modesty that *The Legend of Buratai Volume 2* is a book that is worthy of reading from cover to cover. This is so particularly for those who seek to know how he operated in the situation he found himself. There are so many lessons to learn from the book and I believe it will go a long way in motivating and transforming field Commanders as well as young officers. His enviable life story, miraculous escape from enemy attempts on his life and leadership by example are what prominently portrayed him as a legendary leader.

It is worthy to mention at this stage that the General was

once a school teacher before he enrolled into the Nigerian Army. He was a great sportsman and historian. It is also interesting to note that in this book, we are brought to see that the General is a poet and a meticulous writer of prose. Nigerians, especially young people must retrace their steps and embrace the old school-age of leisure through reading for knowledge and general exposure.

The Legend of Buratai Volume 2, is a book that will not only help Nigerians to better understand the personality of General Buratai and his antecedents but will also go a long way in helping our youths to learn about the disciplines behind success and virtues that can make them to excel in their various endeavors. One of the key secrets of General Buratai's successes is Diligence. He is a man of diligence.

Of particular interest to me is the poem he wrote titled *Are You A Terrorist*. With its unique characteristics of timeliness, the poem addresses the security challenges (insurgency and terrorism) bedeviling our dear country.

This poem calls for self-evaluation by each and every Nigerian. The fact that Mr. Best Agbese's rendition of the poem is also part of the book makes it easier for the reader to understand the poem and its implications to Countering Violent Extremism (CVE).

I have interacted with the General for a long time and I can say that his modesty, diligence, perseverance, courage, loyalty and passion for excellence are what contributed to making him a legendary leader. It is significant to note that,

Nigeria has not witnessed such serious security challenge since the Nigerian Civil War which took place between July 1967 to January 1970. It offered the General the opportunity to prove himself and he did exemplary. This could not have been possible without winning the trust and confidence of President Muhammadu Buhari, Commander-in-Chief of the Armed Forces of the Federal Republic of Nigeria. Today, General Buratai is the longest serving Chief of Army Staff in the history of the Nigerian Army because of his exemplary leadership and gallantry in leading the Army to protect Nigerians and defend the territorial integrity of Nigeria. It is against this backdrop that I want to commend him for finding time to write this memoir which is going to be of immeasurable benefit to the military today and the future generation. It is a masterpiece and I strongly recommend it to officers and men of the Nigerian military as well as young people who seek to know the early life, stages, obstacles and challenges Tukur passed through to become General Buratai. Happy reading.

Major General Paul Tarfa mni (Rtd), Abuja.

"First comes thought; then organisation of that thought, into ideas and plans; then transformation of those plans into reality. The beginning, as you will observe, is in your imagination."

Napoleon Hill

CHAPTER ONE

❖ ❖ ❖

In THE BeGInnInG

In the early 18th century, a young man by the name of Yakurku emerged as a famous warrior and hunter in the land of Hawul. He was renowned for his courage and generosity. My maternal grandparents and the local chief and his council in Buratai heard about the fame of this man and his good deeds. It was therefore with great joy that they received and welcomed him when he came to the land of Buratai. He was given some land to stay in and asked to contribute to the development of the chiefdom, and he obliged them. He would eventually nurture a group of warriors and hunters in Buratai.

This man and his lineage were never troublesome, always peaceful. They never made any attempt to usurp the authority of the traditional chief, because treachery and betrayal were never part of them. They were loyal by nature, reserved to some extent and always said

With Alhaji Ibrahim, my elder
brother, in Maiduguri in the late 60s

As a young student in
TC Potiskum

little. Yakurku was a tall man, athletic in stature and
dark in complexion, and he smiled a lot. He was a
disciplined man and always stood for what he believed
was right. There was much semblance between him
and Yamtarawala, except that the latter established a
dynasty, whereas Yakurku did not.

He married a local girl in Buratai and together they
produced five children, one of which was Yusufu.
Yusufu was my father, and he was the one who joined
the Royal West African Frontier Force (RWAFF) in
1942 and fought gallantly in the Second World War.
My father joined the RWAFF at the age of eighteen.
His enlistment into the RWAFF took him to places like
Lagos, Cotonou (Benin Republic), Mombassa (Kenya),
Cape Town (South Africa), Bombay (India), Lahore
(Pakistan) and Burma, or what some people now call

Myanmar. He was among the soldiers guarding the RWAFF ship, which was constantly on the move.

My father served in the RWAFF as a diligent, obedient and brave soldier. He was loyal to his superiors and even though far away from his family in Buratai, he made it a habit to send them the little money he received as salary to take care of themselves. I believe he was the first person to join the RWAFF in Buratai. One of his four brothers at the time eventually got the name 'Mai Pan' as a sobriquet because he was the only person in Buratai who was always seen with the British Pound Sterling. My father was constant and regular in sending part of his monthly wages to his family in Nigeria. This is a lesson that I hold dear to my heart and I encourage every officer and soldier to learn from this: you must take care of your family

As a young student in TC Potiskum

With my father, Baba Yusufu sitting on a wheelchair. Standing to his right is the Bangladesh Chief of Army Staff, General Belal Shafi ul-Huq

members, because without family we are nothing. My father made sure that he visited Buratai when he was on pass, and most people in Buratai as at that time saw him as a local celebrity.

When the RWAFF was disbanded in 1960, my father got involved in the development of the community. He was respected at the court of the local chief because of his character, exposure and integrity. The grandson of the District Head of Buratai, Alhaji Lawan Maina Barka, who is the current Galadima of Buratai, told me some things about my father that I think I should repeat here:

> I was reliably informed by my father and Baba Yusuf himself about matters of historical importance that had to do with the development of education and the traditional leadership council in Buratai. Baba Yusuf was fortunate enough to join the Army at a very tender age, which gave him the rare opportunity of travelling all over the world. His father was a warrior and a brave hunter who migrated from parts of Hawul to the land of Buratai. He came to Buratai as a youth and my ancestors

With the the author of "The Legend of Buratai Volume 1"
(Dr. Abubakar MS) at my office in 2019

Alhaji Lawan Maina Buratai the Galadiman Buratai is not just a local prince in Buratai but also a close friend and my classmate at TC Potis-kum. In fact, I nominated him as class monitor when the Form Master decided to appoint a new class monitor. Prince Barka, Atanda and myself were all classmates at TC Potiskum.

took an interest in him. He was tall and athletic, with thick eyebrows and gentle demeanour, and he walked like a king. They wasted no time in giving him one of their daughters as a wife. The marriage was blessed with five children, of whom I can remember Mallam Mai Pan and Baba Yusufu, the World War II veteran.

When Baba Yusuf was demobilized from the Army, he came back home and continued to serve the community in Buratai. He was a highly respected member at court, or at least that was what my father told me. Baba Yusuf himself testified to me that he served the community as a sort of liaison with the British colonial masters. Whenever they came to Buratai to discuss any business with the Chief, they had to go through Baba Yusuf because he was the only one in the entire village who could speak English. No one at the palace could communicate in English, and this made him a very powerful and critical stakeholder in the local administration of Buratai. But Baba Yusufu never saw this as a means to take advantage of my grandfather and other princes; he was loyal to the core and served them to the best of his ability. If he had been the ambitious and treacherous type, he could have upstaged my grandfather and taken over the mantle of leadership, because he had all it took to lead the people: the military experience, the language advantage, the warrior gene and a wider network of friends. Instead he chose to serve as a loyal member of the court.

It is good, I tell you, that Buratai used to be the headquarters of all Babur people and we used to have a Hakimi long before Miringa town, but our people are warriors, independent, and hardly tolerate nonsense. When the King of Biu sent one of his sons from Sakwa to come to Buratai as Hakimi, he ruled with an iron fist and oppressed the people. The people of Buratai became angry and made the town ungovernable to the cruel Hakimi. Hakimi was struck down with leprosy, which made Hakimi travel regularly to Biu for treatment.

Hakimi used to stop over at Miringa on his way to and from Biu. The means of transportation at the time were horses for the royalty and donkeys for the peasants. Eventually he told his father, the King, that he would be happy if he was allowed to establish his court and stay in Miringa, because he suspected the people of Buratai to be the cause of his leprosy. His request to stay in Miringa was granted, and that was how the traditional leadership left Buratai for the town of Miringa.

Primary One pupils of Anguwar Sarkin Musulmi Primary school, Kaduna, class of 1968. I am in the front row by the right sitting on the ground with legs crossed

With my teachers and classmates at TC Potiskum (The arrow indicates my exact sitting position).

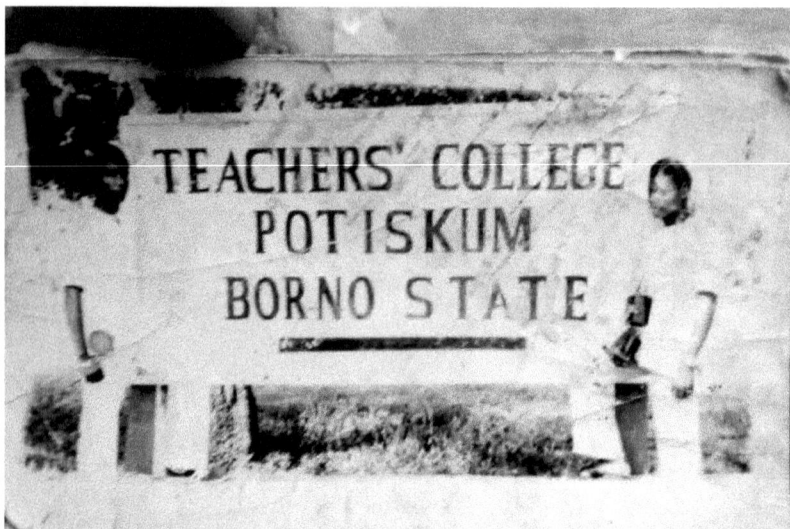

John Atanda (standing on the left) and a class mate in TC Potiskum

The traditional leadership tussle in Buratai became tense and heated until the time when a sole administrator was imposed there. This sole administrator ruled for about 30 years until Baba Yusufu and a few others took the lead to correct this anomaly and saw to it that my family was restored to leadership.

I remember something that happened after Baba Yusufu left the Army and came back to settle in Buratai. As I told you earlier, he was highly respected in court, so the two of them used to go and represent Buratai in Miringa at the Hakimi's court. During one such meeting, Baba Yusuf stood up and told the Hakimi and his council that he wanted to discuss a matter of urgent importance. He was permitted to speak.

He said, "I am worried because of something that I consider very important and I don't think I can hold it in my mind. We, the people of Buratai, are ahead of the village of Gunda, but today as I speak to you, Gunda has a primary school to cater for its children but we in Buratai do not. Therefore, I am appealing to His Highness to provide a school for us in Buratai so that our children can also benefit from modern education. I have travelled and seen what education can do to any community, so Buratai can't afford to stay without a school."

The Hakimi and his council told him that Buratai had been ignored because of the insubordinate nature of its people, but if the people could build a school, Miringa would see to it that teachers were sent to Buratai to teach the children. Baba Yusufu returned to Buratai and told my grandfather all that had transpired in Miringa. My grandfather was happy with the matter and a decision was taken to ask all the wards of Buratai to contribute bricks, mortar, thatch, sticks and poles and so on to build the school.

A man known as Dlangwar took this clarion call seriously, and even though he did not have a son, he made sure that he contributed his quota. Dlangwar fathered three beautiful daughters: Gimbiya, Shatu and Jummai. He went to his farm and gathered enough thatch to roof the school. He tied it into five bundles and put a bundle on

I am first from right, bending down with cap on my head, with some of my mates at TC Potiskum

each of his three daughters, after which he put two bundles on his own head. He led his three daughters to the palace of my grandfather and put down the five bundles of thatch. Then he spoke the following words to my grandfather:

"I heard that you asked that everyone in the community should contribute towards the building of a school, which I believe is a good thing. Here is my contribution for this project, and although I don't have a son, I believe that one day I will have a grandson who will benefit from education and help this community."

He inspired a lot of people to bring in their own donations and eventually the school was built, after which teachers were sent from Miringa to teach our children. Today all of these prophetic statements have been fulfilled in front of our very eyes. There is a romantic dimension to this story. One of these three daughters, Shatu, ended up marrying Baba Yusufu. Shatu was the mother of Tukur and his brethren.

But I am of the opinion that the emergence of Tukur was part of a prediction and prayer by the late Emir of Biu, Mai Mustapha Aliyu. Mai Mustapha said that only God would wipe away the tears of Biu and that God would do this using a son of the soil in His own time. He said that this unique individual would restore the dignity of Biu and bring glad tidings to Nigeria as a whole. I believe that General Tukur Buratai is the fulfilment of this prayer.

There are those who believe that the first person to see the seed of greatness in Tukur was an Indian whom we simply remember as Mr Sylvester. I should like to say that Tukur and I attended the same school in Potiskum, that is the Teachers' College. I remember that when our class monitor was removed because of incompetency and a replacement was needed, Tukur stood in the class and nominated me! The whole class supported his motion, and that was how I became the class monitor.

As I said earlier, one of our expatriate teachers at the school was an Indian national we simply knew as Mr Sylvester. He taught us Philosophy of Education. He was an excellent teacher, but almost all our classmates remember him because of one thing. This man was fond of saying Tukur would be a great man in the future. Isn't it strange? Of all of us that were in the class, it was Tukur that this man singled out for greatness. What informed him to say that?

"Where is Tukur?" said Mr Sylvester one day when he came and discovered that Tukur wasn't yet in the class. "You need to go and call him to come and join the class or else I won't teach. I want to teach the boy who will be great in the future." This transpired in the late 70s. I agree with those who said that Mr Sylvester saw or knew something about Tukur.

I am fortunate enough to have been born into a family of great warriors and leaders who always want to sacrifice for the community. My leadership qualities started to show when I was appointed Captain of Kaigama House in Teacher's College Potiskum. I was firm but merciful and considerate of the younger and the weak students. It was there that I learnt about the importance of justice, courage and mercy in leadership.

My maternal grandfather, Dlangwar, and his three daughters, Gimbiya, Shatu and Jummai, taking thatch to the chief's palace as part of their contribution to the building of the first primary school in Buratai. Shatu would later marry my father and give birth to me. May Allah grant her paradise.

My grandfather Yakurku, the great hunter and warrior.

✎ LESSON ✎

Be proud of your roots and always be obedient to your parents and teachers or instructors. To be great, you must humble yourself to learn from those who want to teach you what you need to know. Don't forget the fact that I benefited immensely from the positive proclamations of Mr Sylvester.

"You! What is best for
you is the Army."

Lt. Colonel Muhammadu Buhari,1976

CHAPTER TWO

❖ ❖ ❖

Dr Gidado Kumo speaks

S omething symbolic happened to the people of
the North-Eastern state in 1975. It was symbolic
because it was the first opportunity President
Muhammadu Buhari got to go to the North-East
as a leader for in that year General Murtala Ramat
Mohammed appointed him to serve as governor of the
North-Eastern state from August 1975 all through to
March 1976.

After completing our elementary schools, we were
admitted into Borno Teachers' College, Maiduguri
in November 1974. We all came from different
backgrounds. Tukur is from the southern parts of Borno
state, although he lived and stayed in Maiduguri and
speaks Kanuri. I am from Kumo town in Gombe state
but went to elementary school in Maiduguri. Tukur is
Babur by tribe and I am Fulbe. We connected easily at
school because that was how God meant it to be. It was

a boarding school with good infrastructure. The school has now been converted to Sir Kashim Ibrahim College of Education. Our set included people like Aminu Turaki, Ibrahim Haruna, Samuel Bulus, Asuquo, to mention but a few. What made my relationship with Tukur outstanding was that we shared the same dorm and class, to be precise Form 1B. We had a state-of-the-art sport facility, good accommodation and excellent meals. I developed an interest in volleyball and hockey right from the first day I joined the school. Although Tukur and others, like Aminu Turaki, would later be transferred to Teachers' College Potiskum, I still stayed in touch with him. We corresponded together every now and then and sustained our relationship through all the years that have gone by.

Perhaps I should give the reason Tukur and others like Aminu Turaki were moved to Potiskum. There was a protest by some students against the new UPE policy introduced by the government of General Olusegun Obasanjo. I was certain that Tukur was not in school when the protest took place, but because of his vocal nature and roughneck disposition, some teachers thought he was among those who participated in the protest.

One of those teachers, Mallam Tanko Gwoza, came to the class and asked us if Tukur was among those who had organised, led or participated in the protest. I told him that Tukur had not participated in the protest because he was ill and had been given a pass to go home for treatment. The teacher refused to believe what I said and went ahead to include Tukur's name among the protesters. He was therefore an innocent victim but he took it in good faith and left for Potiskum.

An important event happened in November, 1975 at Borno Teachers' College, but it escaped Tukur's memory until the year 2020 when I brought it to his notice. This event took place when we were in Form 2. It involved the then Lieutenant Colonel Muhammadu Buhari, who was then the Military Governor of the North-Eastern State, and Tukur Yusuf. Life! Everything is interconnected; it is just that we don't have eyes to see and minds to fathom the future, otherwise we would all be cautious and careful about how we live our lives. It was President Muhammdu Buhari who first said Tukur should join the Army, that he was fit for it. His words were what ignited the passion for soldiering in Tukur.

Who would think or believe that Tukur would join the Army and eventually be appointed by President Buhari as the Chief of Army Staff of Nigeria? None of us in Borno Teachers' College could think about that, because we were young and naive. As for our teachers, most of them couldn't perceive the seeds of greatness that were in us. They took us for granted! I would like to say that it was not just our teachers; even some of our parents didn't have high expectations of us. But look at us today. I am a PhD holder and Tukur is a General in the Army. I was a boisterous individual who could also be described as a maverick right from our schooldays. I don't think I have changed; I am still boisterous, very brash and straightforward.

Lt. Col. Muhammadu Buhari was posted to North-Eastern State as Military Governor in 1975 and he stayed as Governor until March 1976. This new governor was different; very down to earth, tall and lanky, with thick eyebrows, a small moustache and gap-toothed. He used to come to our school in the evenings to watch students doing sports activities, and was fond of watching volleyball and football. He used to come to the school in the company of two people who I now realised might be his Aide de Camp and Military Assistant. None of them ever visited the school in military fatigues; they were always in mufti. Lt. Col. Buhari used to sit on the boot of his official Peugeot 504 saloon and watch students play sports. I believe he loves children as well as sports.

One day a ball flew off the volleyball court and Tukur went to retrieve it and on his way back with it, he threw it with full force and it hit a youth called Samuel Bulus. The military governor saw the way Tukur had thrown the ball and how it hit Samuel. He called Tukur and said something that I now believe is prophetic. He said "You should join the Army because of your toughness and strength. See how you hit the ball so hard that it nearly injured your mate when it hit him?"

He said it in Hausa, which is the lingua franca of the North. The exact words he used to address him were "*Maganin ka soja yaro!*" He was a young man of 34 in 1976 and Tukur was just 16 years old, but that was the first time their paths crossed. He took notice of Tukur's build, assertive stance, cocky and bumptious attitude, and like a prophet, he predicted that what was best for Tukur was the Army. I remember that at that time Tukur was a roughneck who was fearless and ready to fight to defend the honour of his mates.

I cannot really say if what he said subconsciously caused Tukur to be drawn to the Army, but I know it increased his self-confidence as a potential soldier, because if Lt. Col. Buhari, who happened to be the most senior military officer in the region, could say that what was best for Tukur was the Army, then Tukur must have felt he was good for it. Still, there are times I wonder about fate and destiny, and how it affects us. Garth Nix said, "Does the walker choose the path, or the path the walker?" I think in the case of Tukur, the path chose the walker. Many people will give different answers to this question, but that's okay.

Today that young military governor is the democratically-elected president of Nigeria, while the 16-year-old boy is an Army general and Chief of Army Staff of the Nigerian Army, yet both of them have forgotten about their historical encounter in 1976. Guy Gavriel Kay said: "There are no wrong turnings, only paths we had not known we were meant to walk." I believe the President will remember this story after some reflection.

Someone is behind all of these happenings; the Hand of omnipotence and omniscience guided and planned Lt. Col. Muhammadu Buhari's posting to Maiduguri in 1975, meeting with Tukur at Borno Teachers' College, Maiduguri, his eventual return as a civilian president, his visit to the headquarters of the MNJTF in Chad and his appointment of this same boy he met in 1976 (now known as General Buratai) as his Chief of Army staff. I believe God is behind these two eminent Nigerians and that our duty as citizens is to rally behind them and pray for them to discharge their duties with the fear of God and in sincerity. Condemning the president and the Army to the extent of ridiculing and blackmailing them is counterproductive and dangerous, because it will incur God's displeasure. My advice to them, especially my schoolmate and friend, Tukur, is to continue to remain humble and be just in the discharge of his duties.

My first encounter with President Buhari was when he was posted to Borno as a governor. I was a JSS One student at that time, and he used to come to our school in the evenings to watch us play football. It was on one such visit that he said that what was best for me was to join the Army.

❧ LESSON ❧

People should know that nothing happens in this life by chance or coincidence; there is no such thing as coincidence. Everything that had happened or is happening is carefully arrange and designed by Allah, who had planned everything to fulfil His eternal plan. We are all inter-connected but most of us don't really know. Indeed, Martin Luther Jr. got it right when he wrote: "In a real sense all life is inter-related. All men are caught in an inescapable network of mutuality, tied in a single garment of destiny. Whatever affects one directly, affects all indirectly. I can never be what I ought to be until you are what you ought to be, and you can never be what you ought to be until I am what I ought to be."

Don't be in a hurry to condemn someone because he doesn't do what you do or think as you think or as fast There was a time when you didn't know what you know today."

Malcolm X

CHAPTER THree

❖ ❖ ❖

JOHn ATanDa speaKS

My name is John Olabisi Atanda and I am Yoruba by tribe. I am also a devout Christian and a family man. I work as a high school teacher and school Administrator in Yobe and I was born, raised and schooled in Potiskum. I still reside with my family in Potiskum, although my workplace is in Nguru town.

A lot of people don't know that before Tukur became an Army officer and a historian, he was a teacher. I met him in the 70s as a classmate in Teachers' College, Potiskum. I should like to say that Tukur is not just a classmate to me but a brother and a close friend. A lot of qualities attracted me to him, but I think his charity, generosity, calmness and most especially his religious tolerance impressed me the most. Tukur is an exceptional human being from TC, Potiskum. He is just different, always at ease with himself, a bit reserved

Mr. John Olabisi Atanda. Atanda is a career teacher who has contributed to the development of education in Yobe state.

and smiles when he is happy or pleased with your comments. He does not say no to a friend and he can go the extra mile to please his friends and associates.

Even though he doesn't have royal blood flowing in his veins, Tukur comports himself like a prince. There is a grace and decorum you see around him when he walks, talks or looks at you. I think that was why he was made a House Captain at TC, Potiskum. I can remember he was the House Captain of Kaigama House. He was a popular figure at the school. Tukur was fair and resolute, and he treated junior students like his younger brothers.

I have always known that he would be a great person in Nigeria, so when I heard that a children's story book titled *The Legend of Buratai* had been written in his honour, I smiled in satisfaction. There is no way this man won't end up as a legend; his virtues are those of a legend. I believe that regardless of the profession he chooses, he will end up as a leader and a legend. Why did I say so? Because his courage, diligence, sense of purpose, fairness and willingness to sacrifice for others are the things that all great leaders and legends are made of.

Some of us who were fortunate enough to be his classmates knew that Tukur was different from us, because of the weird remarks and comments of one of our teachers, Mr P. C. Sylvester. Mr Sylvester was an expatriate teacher from India, and I think he was Hindu, because I can remember the red scarf he used to tie on his hand and how he used to touch it before he started to teach. Of all the students in TC Potiskum,

Mr Sylvester took special interest in only one person: Tukur. I recall him saying, "Tukur, you are going to be a great man and a leader in your country."

He would pause during a class, or sometimes before the commencement of a class, while he made the above remarks. He was serious about it, as if he was a prophet. There were times he said to us that he would not start to teach the class until Tukur was present. At such times the class monitor would run out to go and look for him. By the way, Tukur was always a punctual student but sometimes prefects come to the class late because of their duties.

I don't know the whereabouts of Mr Sylvester today, but all of us who were classmates of Tukur in TC Potiskum knew about this man and his prophetic declarations to Tukur. I can't really say whether Tukur believed him or not as of then, but I think he has now realised that the weird man was truly right.

My first memorable encounter with Tukur happened in 1979, if I am correct. I was looking for an empty store in the school to convert it into a room. I wasn't a prefect, but as a senior student I could have a separate corner for myself. Tukur and most of the prefects had their private corners at the school.

When I approached Tukur and told him about my need, he obliged and said, "Let's go round to search for the kind of place you want." Unfortunately for me, we searched everywhere but couldn't find a place for me to convert into a room. I was sad and downcast. Tukur was not happy that I was disappointed. He was really an empathetic student, and he is still full of empathy. He was quiet, and then after a few minutes he said, "John, why don't you just come to my place and let's share the room together? We can get something to partition it into two. But you will not bring another person there. Only the two of us."

I was flabbergasted when I heard that. I said, "You mean I should share your place with you?"

He said, "Yes, of course!"

That was how I relocated to his place and the two of us became room-mates. He received me with open arms and made me feel as comfortable as if I was his brother. He was then not just a Muslim but the President of the school's Muslim Students' Society (M.S.S.), yet he received me even though I am a Christian and a southerner. I think he was blind to all forms of religious bias.

I vividly remember that occasionally he would bring out his Qur'an and tell me to also come with my Bible so that we could do comparative study on Christianity and Islam with a view to better understanding each other's perspective. He would quote the Qur'an as well as portions of the Bible to support his argument and where I was right, he would accept my belief, but whenever it came to the issue of God having a son, he would stand his ground and say it was wrong. He would quote some portion of the Qur'an, especially *suratul Ikhlas*, and I would get upset and angry with him. Once I was upset with the outcome of our argument, I would simply park my Bible and other study materials out of anger because of the way he had attacked one of my cardinal beliefs. During such a moment, he would only smile and say: "John, calm down, we are not fighting."

He was very tolerant of me and my attitude. If he was angry with me in any way, he never showed it.

My relationship with Tukur got so intimate that whenever my girlfriends sent me letters, I would show them to him to hear his opinion of the letter and the writer. There were times when after he finished reading the letter, he would tell me that the girl who wrote it was intelligent. I used to share all my secrets with him, not just because we were close but also because Tukur knew how to keep secrets. Whatever confidential talk you had with him stayed between the two of you; he was not a blabbermouth at all. He was a serious student who was well respected by both students and teachers. I can't remember any time I saw him quarrelling or fighting with anyone in the school. He was the kind of person who minded his own business. He was also a contented student who liked to live within his means.

He was a voracious reader. We sat for the Teachers' Grade 3 and Grade 2 exams together, and both of us performed well and graduated in 1980. I stayed in Potiskum with my family while he left for Maiduguri to join his. We lost contact with each other, and at that time such luxuries as mobile phones were not in existence.

In 1981, because he knew my family house in Potiskum, he paid me a surprise visit. I was washing my clothes at home when I heard the footsteps of someone walking like a soldier towards me. It was rather strange because I could not remember any military association with my family. I paused and raised my head to see who was coming. To my surprise it was Tukur in his cadet's fatigues. We were both happy to meet each other and we connected with each other very easily. He told me

31

that he was now in the Nigerian Defence Academy (NDA) as a cadet, and I should come and join him. No one would ever believe that the gentle, religious and easy-going Tukur would join the Army, but here was he doing that which Providence had designed for him. I couldn't believe it – Tukur, now a cadet! He stayed for a while and we went to town together so that he could say hello to some classmates who were also staying in Potiskum. He is the kind of person who treasures relationships and friendship with old friends.

At one point, we lost touch with each other for a very long time, until I met one of our classmates, who told me Tukur had gone to Bangladesh for a course. He said I should wait for him to return if I wanted to see him. I tried to reach him in Bangladesh but didn't succeed, so I gave up.

When he returned from Bangladesh and was promoted to the rank of brigadier, he came to my family house in Potiskum. I was no longer living there because I had got married and moved out. He came and asked my family members about me, and they told him I had moved out. He gave them his business card and asked them to pass it to me, saying I should try to link up with him.

Not long after that, my wife came to the family house for a visit. She was told about what happened and given Tukur's business card to deliver to me. When she brought it, I discovered that he was now a brigadier – Brigadier General Tukur Yusuf Buratai! I was impressed with his meritorious rise to the top and I also considered it a thing of joy that my school roommate was now one of the top military brass. I wasted no time in dialling the mobile number I saw on the business card. He answered after one dial. I was thrilled to hear his soft, gentle voice on the other side. I skipped all the formalities and the pleasantries. I decided to play a riddle on him. I said, "Tukur."

He said, "Yes."

I said, "Yusuf."

He said, "Yes, that's me."

I paused for some seconds and said, "Buratai."

He said, "Yes."

So I said, "Can you guess the identity of who is talking to you?"

He said he couldn't, but I should please save his time and provide the answer to my riddle.

I said, "This is John Olabisi Atanda, your friend at T.C. Potiskum."

Before I could barely finish, he exploded with joy and told me that he had been looking for me all this while. He asked about my situation and the well-being of my family. He was so excited to hear from me. His new status and power had not changed him. He was still humble, reasonable and empathetic. He told me that he was now in Port Harcourt as a Brigade Commander. He said that the then Chief of Army Staff was coming to Port Harcourt to commission one of their projects, so I should come there as a guest. I politely declined the invitation because my wife was terminally ill at that time and there was no way I could leave her alone and go to Port Harcourt. I narrated my ordeal to him and he understood. He asked me if there was any challenge, and told him that the hospital bill was beyond my capacity.

He said, "Is it okay if I come in to assist so that your wife can get treated in time?"

I said, "Of course, yes."

I think it was God who used him to save my wife, because I couldn't raise the money the hospital was demanded from me.

He asked for my account details and transferred the exact amount the hospital asked for. He is such a kind-hearted person.

We have been communicating through SMS, but we haven't seen each other face to face yet. I don't want to bother him because I know he is now a busy man. In fact, I am somewhat scared to come close to him. He is now the Chief of Staff of the Nigerian Army and his hands are full because of the numerous modern security challenges this country is confronted with.

All of our classmates are proud of him and the majority of us still remember what Mr Sylvester said to him in T.C. Potiskum. Some of us told him to look for Mr Sylvester and I think he tried to look for the whereabouts of the man or his relatives, but so far all his efforts have yielded no results.

Whenever I look back at how we started in Potiskum and juxtapose it with the present status of Tukur, a verse of the Bible comes to my mind: 'Despise not the beginning of little things for though thy beginning be small, thy latter end shall be great.'

The Tukur I once knew no longer exists. He has been transformed into a legendary General saddled with the onerous task of defending Nigeria from external aggression and low-intensity conflicts like insurgency and banditry. I knew how bad the situation in the north-east was before he took over as Chief of Army Staff. I am still living in Potiskum with my wife and children. We know what we experienced in 2013 and 2014, not just in Potiskum but places like Gujba, Gaidam, Damaturu, Maiduguri, Mubi, Yola, Dikwa, Ngamboru and so on. The insurgents were literally in charge because they had the upper hand. They detonated explosives with reckless abandon, ransacked towns and villages with ease, terrorised innocent civilians like myself, burnt down churches, massacred harmless schoolchildren and kidnapped women and girls. Some of us contemplated relocating to other places because of the fear and uncertainty, but the emergence of General Buratai changed everything in the northeast. Potiskum is now as calm and peaceful as it used to be, and commerce is thriving.

I believe that Tukur's decision to join the Army was divine and I am happy that he is providing credible leadership to the Army to ensure there is peace in Nigeria.

∾ LESSON ∾

Young people of today should try to understand that success is not something that happens overnight but is an accumulation of habitual excellence and persistence. Secondly, they should know that they must transcend the ethno-religious divide if they want to excel and be reckoned as legends. To enter into the league of legends, they must be ready to serve humanity and not just those of their own religious or ethnic affiliation. All legendary leaders take risks to make others happy; they go out of their way to ensure that justice and mercy are enthroned in their sphere of influence. This is what Tukur stands for: justice and mercy.

"It is a proud privilege to be a soldier – a good soldier [with] discipline, self-respect, pride in his unit and his country, a high sense of duty and obligation to comrades and to his superiors, and a self-confidence born of demonstrated ability."

George S. Patton Jr.

CHAPTER Four

❖ ❖ ❖

Destiny and The Army

I was commissioned on the 17th of December 1983, and that was when I started my military career as a Second Lieutenant with the new adjustment in the Service. I was posted to 82 Division of the Nigerian Army where I was further posted to 26 Battalion, Nigerian Army in Elele in Rivers State.

I would say that there were many memorable moments while serving in the Nigerian Army. The one very important thing that I always cherish was that I wrote all my examinations and passed in one sitting and got all my promotions when due. And to crown it all was this key appointment as the Chief of Army Staff, which is indeed the aspiration of every commissioned officer in the Nigerian Army. This was not just Buratai alone; every officer wants to reach the zenith of his career, which is to become the COAS. So I give glory to Almighty Allah and I thank Mr. President, my

The portrait of President Buhari then as Major General Muhammadu Buhari,Head of State of Nigeria inspired me to cherish the virtues of discipline andintegrity as a young officer who just got commissioned in December 1983.

Commander-in-Chief, President Muhammadu Buhari, who deemed it fit to appoint me as the Chief of Army Staff. The aspiration of every commission officer is not only to become a general but to become the Chief of Army Staff.

My name is Tukur—Tukur Yusufu Buratai, but most people know me as General Buratai or simply Buratai. Buratai is a word derived from the Babur-Bura language and it is today a proper noun referring to a village not far from Biu town. Buratai is one of the

Explaining an important aspect of the warfare to my
Commander-in-Chief in Maiduguri

oldest districts of Biu Kingdom which is the home of
the Bura people which was existing before the advent of
Yamtarawala. The name Buratai was originally derived
from Buratai which in Kanuri is catch the Bura people.
This happened during the period of slave raiding. The
original Buratai settlement was established by two
gallant brothers named Dawai and Yagay. It is near
the Hyena Mountain (Gar Mabulu in Babur-Bura),
about 38 km away from Biu along Damaturu-Biu
road. However, in recent history, the more popularly
known Buratai settlements are Kufi Buratai and the
present Buratai town. Kufi Buratai was abandoned
when the people moved en mass to the present Buratai
town. Kufi Buratai is virtually a relic. The history of
Buratai is interwoven with that of Miringa through the
ruling dynasty. Tradition has it that when Yamtarawala
first came to Biu land from Ngazargamu he met only

As officer cadet with MM Adamu

the villages of Limbur, Diwa, Miringa and Buratai but when he attempted to invade Buratai the people escaped his trap and foiled his move.

I understand that Tukur is originally an Arabic name, and some people said that it was Muhammadu Tukur who ruled Kano from 1893 to 1894 that made the name popular. From what I gathered, the name means *extraordinary*. I was named Tukur in honour of the Lawan of Gunda village, who used to be my father's confidant and religious teacher. They called him Lawan Tukur Gunda. He was well versed in Islamic jurisprudence, theology and Arabic, and my father benefited from his advanced knowledge of the religion. After my father returned from the war, he took great interest in matters of religion and faith, and God linked him up with Lawan Tukur to help him in his quest for knowledge. To show how much he revered and respected Lawan Tukur, he named me after the man as a sign of honour.

REMINISCENCE

apt TY Buratai High Jump Borno
ate Contingent 1989 National
oorts Festival Lagos

As a captain displaying my talent in high jump at the 1989 National Sports Festival in Lagos. I was part of the Borno contingent that performed well at the event and won medals.

Back in the days when I was a high school student, my English tutor told me that one of the rewards of hard work and diligence is a good reputation, and that a good reputation will always promote or elevate you in life. It will surely and certainly help you to mingle and interact with kings. A reputation has the ability to transform a complete nonentity into a star, or celebrity might be a better word.

Now this is what fascinated me. My teacher said celebrities were always known by their first name or surname, or in some instances a name that was usually not more than three syllables. I didn't take this celebrity thing seriously, because although I cherish hard work, diligence and excellence in my pursuits, I never wanted to be a celebrity. I am naturally a shy person, very private, someone who doesn't like the crowd. Like most young people of today, I didn't know that hard work, diligence and excellence will always make an ordinary fellow to be extraordinary. I think this is the reason why most people call me Buratai, even though there are scores of individuals — dead and alive — who have the same surname.

I am today the single individual synonymous with Buratai, to such an extent that once you mention the name, I am the first thing that comes to the minds of people. People get flabbergasted when I tell them my first name is Tukur, Tukur Yusufu Buratai, and that Buratai is the name of my village. Everything about me starts or emanates from that village. I was born there. I started going to school there too.

Students of Bill and Samuel School, Abuja and the author of *The Legend of Buratai Volume One* when Sprezzatura Publishing organized a book reading at the school.

I am a Nigerian from the village of Buratai in the Biu Local Government Area. Biu is also an Emirate Council with a first-class chief and it has a population of over a million people. I understand that an old sage predicted my coming some four hundred years before I was born. The old sage told the Great Yamtarawala that three great men would emerge in Biu Kingdom, one every hundred years after his demise. He told him this in the year 1555 and the Great Yamtarawala died shortly after, in 1560.

I don't know much about the three great men who emerged in 1660, 1760 and even 1860, but I guess most of them appeared from his direct bloodline, while a few might have been military commanders who led different battles to protect and preserve Biu Kingdom. It is unfortunate that we don't have written documentation that chronicles their history, but stories abound in oral narratives.

What surprised me the most was that I didn't know that I was also a child of prophecy. The old sage told the Great Yamtarawala that while three great men would emerge in Biu Kingdom every hundred years after his demise, a single individual would emerge in the four hundredth year. That means that it is only a single individual would emerge in 1960, for the year 1960 is exactly four hundred years after the demise of the Great King. It might be that my ancestors were among those who followed Prince Abdullahi, who later became known as Yamtarawala from Ngazargamu of the Kanem Borno Empire to Biu land in 1525, or he might have met with my ancestors in Buratai village and proceeded to forge a strong affinity with them through intermarriage. Whatever might have been the case, I understand that my birth was predicted long before I was born.

There are things that fascinate me whenever I read the history of Yamtarawala. For example, Cohen (1988) described him in superlative terms:

Yampta not only was a powerful hunter and fighter (in warfare) but had strong magical-sorcerer powers as well. The local Bura people were such good fighters that he wanted their secret. He befriended a local girl, and she told him of the secret charm that gave her people this fighting power. He stole the secret talisman and became famous as a fighter, hunter, and source of magical power. He then became a leader.

I don't think it is a coincidence that I also love hunting, the esoteric, and self-sacrifice for others. The legendary acts and deeds of Yamtarawala had motivated many people like me.

I started my elementary school in Kaduna at Anguwar Sarki Musulmi Primary School in 1967. We stayed for a brief period in Kaduna, where my father worked with the late Alhaji Ibrahim Biu[1] and relocated to the north-east (Maiduguri) when the north-eastern states were created. At least I remember that I spent one term in that school. I later saw my report card as a grown-up youth. When we came to Maiduguri, my father was transferred to the Ministry of Education and worked with the then Commissioner of Education. My father wasted no time in getting me enrolled into a school to continue with my primary school education, because he believed in education. I was enrolled into the Lamisula Primary School as a Primary 1 pupil and I was there until I reached Primary 4, when I was transferred to St. Patrick's, all in Maiduguri.

St. Patrick's Primary School used to be a missionary school just like Wulari One Primary School, but it is now known as Kirikasama Primary School. Kirikasama

---

1. The late Alhaji Ibrahim Biu was the first Minister of Information of the Northern region and he was like the mouthpiece of the North during the time of the Sarduana until 1966. He started his career as a pupil's teacher in 1943 but later went to Kaduna Technical College to get trained as a technician and eventually returned to Biu in 1947 as Resident Engineer. He rose to become Senior Councilor and member of the Council in Charge of Works up until 1956. He ran for election for the Northern House of Parliament in 1956 and won with an overwhelming majority. Although he was much younger than the Sardauna, he was appointed the first indigenous minister of Information. It was said that after the rebellion of 1966, when Major Chukwuma Nzeogwu saw him, he said: "...mouthpiece of the NPC, we looked for you to silence you forever, but now that the rebellion is over, go back to your village and make sure you don't grant any interviews." He was conferred with the National Honors of Commander of the Niger in 1981 and was also turbaned as the Waziri of Biu in 1973.

is a Kanuri word which means the place of sand, or where there is sand, because at that time the area where the school is situated was the place where construction workers used to go and get sand for construction work. All of the sand used to build the Musa Usman State Secretariat complex was fetched from Kirikasama.

Kirikasama Primary School is perhaps the most popular elementary school in Maiduguri because of its strategic location; the school is situated opposite the Musa Usman[2] State Secretariat and is very big. That is where I completed my Primary School education. It was very interesting being in these schools — Anguwar Sarkin Musulmi, Lamisula and Kirikasama. Our teachers were exceptional teachers who taught us with passion and discipline. Their command of the English language and how they taught us Arithmetic was excellent. I completed my primary school in Kirikasama with flying colours and I made my mark there as a boy of good character.

I was admitted into Borno Teachers' College after completing my primary school education at Kirikasama. I can't really say why I got admitted into Teachers' College, but by and large I think the teaching profession was then a noble profession. It was at that time that the Obasanjo administration introduced the Universal Basic Education Policy, so we were the first set of students that started it. That was in 1977. This UBE initiative of the government was vehemently

---

2. Musa Usman was a Brigadier who became the first governor of the North-Eastern State. He was Governor from May 1967 to July 1975 after the state had been formed from part of Northern Region during the military regime of General Yakubu Gowon. Brigadier Usman attended the Royal Military Academy Sandhurst, England gaining his commission in 1962.

criticized and rejected by some students because the whole thing was misunderstood, although some people said it was ill conceived.

Some students at the Teachers' College had made up their minds to continue up to Grade II and not to stop at Grade III. In fact, the Government will eventually scrap off the Teachers Training College and replace them with Colleges of Education, which automatically made the National Certificate in Education (NCE) certificate a recognized qualification for teaching in primary and secondary schools.

Before the advent of the Colleges of Education, we had in Nigeria the Teacher Training Colleges[3] where students were admitted immediately after completing primary school. It is rather unfortunate that many of the NCE graduates of today are worse than Grade II teachers of old[4]. Aficionados of education are saying that the issue of teacher training is something that Nigeria needs to revisit, because at the moment our teachers are performing below average, and this is a result of the kind of training given to them.

---

3. The first institution set up to train teachers came up in 1896, when the Church Missionary Society (CMS), now the Church of Nigeria (Anglican Communion) established St. Andrews Teachers' College, Oyo. This improved the quality of teachers who were hitherto standard six certificate holders. Grade III teachers were then being produced. With time, many more TTCs were established. Baptist Training College, Ogbomosho was established in 1897, followed by St. Paul's Training College, Awka in 1904. In 1905, Oron got Oron Training Institute, just as Ibadan got Wesleyan Training Institute in 1928. In 1929, St. Charles Training College, Onitsha was established. In Northern Nigeria, the government was directly involved in the funding and managing of their Teachers' Colleges. Teachers Training College, Katsina and Toro Teachers' Training College, are clear examples.

4. This assertion was made by Professor Peter Okebukola in an interview with *Vanguard* of 2nd February 2016.

There are instances where students just go to the Colleges of Education simply because they have nowhere else to go and acquire a certificate; they don't have any interest whatsoever in teaching. I agree that the remuneration of teachers is very poor, but that doesn't mean there are no people who truly have passion for the job. One of the advantages of the Teachers' College was that it had the ability to mould teachers from a young age, such that the graduates ended up breathing and talking nothing but teaching. Students moved to Teachers' College immediately after completing primary school and from JSS-1 students would be taught as teachers and not as engineers, doctors or artists.

So the idea of stopping at Grade III met with stiff resistance from such students, and this misunderstanding between the students and the authorities drove some students to organise protests to show their grievance. Of course, one might expect that such a protest would not be allowed by the authorities because it might get out of hand and snowball into a breakdown of law and order.

The authorities got the police to stop the protest and this led to a clash with the students. I was still a youth at that time, but I was fortunate enough to know that we as students don't have the wherewithal to challenge the government. In any case, my father had cautioned me to be law abiding as a student, saying that he would not condone any reckless behaviour from me.

At about that time, some students challenged President Jean Bedel Bokassa of the Central African Republic and the man responded with a strong arm.

This crisis led to the death of some students because the police used live ammunition on them. The incident drew the wrath of the international community, especially France, and it didn't take long for them to come up with what they termed *Operation Barracuda*. Simply put, *Operation Barracuda* was an operation planned and organised by France to overthrow President Bokassa, and it succeeded.

Bokassa himself was not that popular across the continent, and his arrogance was irritating everyone. He went as far as transforming himself from a president into an emperor and declared the whole country as his empire. That incident with the students was badly managed, and it was what led to his downfall. I think the Nigerian authorities at that time were conscious of that incident. They were prepared not to allow any group of students to organise any protest that could easily lead to chaos.

The organisers of the protest were identified, and the authorities decided to move them out of the school to other places, because they reasoned that if they allowed them to continue at the school, they might end up winning over other students to their cause and eventually stage another protest. So the best thing to do was to disband them, to make it impossible for them to plan together. They were, you might say, scattered abroad! Unfortunately, some of us were unlucky enough to be grouped together with those who spearheaded, organised and participated in the protests. We were taken out of the school and sent to various schools within the state. That was how I found myself in Teachers' College Potiskum.

It didn't take me much time to acclimatize to my new surroundings, settle down in Potiskum and continue to behave as a reasonable student. I went about my business without making any trouble in the school. I obeyed my seniors, respected my classmates and revered my teachers as if they were my parents. There were instances where I got annoyed because things didn't go the way I wanted or because someone violated my rights, but I kept my cool. I endured every hardship and discomfort in Potiskum, because I know how to adjust to any surroundings in which I find myself.

I think providence took me to Potiskum to meet a spectacular teacher known as Mr. P.C Sylvester. This man was an Indian expatriate who saw something in me at a time when nobody saw any sign of greatness in me. In fact, I didn't believe in myself as such. But Mr. Sylvester would always refer to me in class as a 'great man'. All my classmates knew this. At some point, I started to feel embarrassed whenever he referred to me as a future great man. It came to the point where if this teacher came to class and saw that I was not present, he would tell the class that he would not teach if Tukur was not around.

"Go and call Tukur, because if the great man is not present, I will not start teaching; I have to wait for the great man," Mr. Sylvester would say.

I completed my Grade II in 1980. One thing that made me very happy and satisfied was my results. I am proud of my Grade II result. I was one of the best students who sat for the Grade II Exams in 1980, and I came out with the best result. All my external papers were "Bs" in the Grade II certificate and all the internal papers were also "As."

So, it wasn't that hard for me to secure admission into a higher institution of learning. I got admitted into the Borno College of Basic Studies (BOCOBS), but as God would have it, destiny had a different plan for me. I quickly settled down at BOCOBS and was preparing for an interview with the Borno State Scholarship Board to help me further my studies.

I spent a term in BOCOBS before something happened that changed the course of my life. I thought and dreamed about different professions that I wanted to join, but the Army was top of the list. The only problem was that I didn't know how to go about it. There was no internet at that time and information was not easily accessible to people especially students like us who couldn't afford to buy newspapers.

One of my friends who happened to graduate from Teachers' College Potiskum a year ahead of me came to me one night at about 8 or 9 p.m. and told me that there was an announcement over the radio that supplementary entrance examination into the Nigerian Defence Academy[5] (NDA) was going to take place the

---

5. The Nigerian Defence Academy (NDA) was established in 1964 to meet the urgent need for an autonomous institution for the training of officer-cadets for the Nigerian Armed Forces. Previously, the Royal Military Academy, Sandhurst, UK and the Indian Academy, mainly provided the necessary military and academic training for the granting of the commission into the Nigerian Armed Forces. The Academic Branch of the NDA basically handles the academic component of training. For purposes of academic training, NDA was, at inception, affiliated to the University of Ibadan. To ensure that proper standards were maintained, the University moderated the then Nigerian Defence Academy Certificate of Education (NDACE) examination which each Cadet was expected to pass as part of the requirements for obtaining a commission. NDACE was rated as the equivalent of the General Certificate of Education (Advanced Level). The degree programme commenced with only 2 Faculties: Faculty of Arts and Social Sciences (FASS) and the Faculty of Science

following day. He came on a Friday and the following Saturday was the entrance exams D-Day. This friend of mine, by name Mamman Mai Lawan, asked my opinion about the NDA; he wanted to know if I was interested in the military.

I told him what was in my mind point blank. I said, "I am truly interested in the Army and would like to sit for the entrance exams."

He had already made up his mind to sit for the exams, but he wanted me to come along. He was a good friend; his courage and confidence encouraged me to sit for the entrance exams. I remember that he came on a motorcycle, and that was how my military career started. I asked about the requirements and he told me all that was needed. Luckily, I had them all with me, because it was at that time that I was also preparing for the scholarship interview. So I had all my credentials with me, but one item was missing; my passport photograph. We went to a photographer, where I had a shot taken, and the following morning we went back and collected it. We rode on his motorcycle to the Maimalari[6] Cantonment, Maiduguri, got accredited and sat for entrance exams inside one of the primary

---

(FS) with a total of 6 academic departments. Currently, this has grown to 4 faculties (Faculty of Arts and Social Sciences (FASS), Faculty of Sciences(FS), Faculty of Engineering (FE) and Faculty of Military Science and Interdisciplinary Studies (FMSIS)) with 18 departments, namely, Accounting and Management, Economics, Geography, History and International Studies, Languages, Political Science and Defence Studies, Psychology, Biological Science, Chemistry, Mathematics, Computer Science, Physics, Civil Engineering, Electrical and Electronic Engineering, Mechanical Engineering, Intelligence and Cyber Security, Logistics and Supply Chain Management, and Military Science and Technology. Nigeria Defence Academy. (2019) NDA Academic Branch Online Available at: https://academics.nda.edu.ng/ (Accessed on 22 September 2019)

6. Maimalari Cantonment, Maiduguri was named after the legendary Brigadier General Zakariya Maimalari who was assassinated in January 1966.

school classes of the Command schools. That was how we wrote the entrance examination.

After about two months or thereabouts, the results of the entrance exams were released by the Academy; luckily I had succeeded, but unfortunately my good friend had not. I was happy that I had made the shortlist, but still sad because my friend, whom God used to deliver the information to me, didn't make it. I consider all that happened as an act of God. In fact, I see it as a miracle. True! That's how I see the whole thing. My friend just came of his own volition — nobody told him that I might be interested in the Army, but I was interested and hoped God would send me help on how to go about the whole thing. He was the answer to my prayers.

This life is full of mysteries and I think there are no coincidences in life; everything is happening for a reason. All the people that cross our paths and the places we go to are not just mere coincidence, but most of us are blind and deaf. We have eyes and ears, but we don't actually see and hear what the Almighty is trying to show or tell us. I still get perplexed whenever I remember that my military career started when I was just about to go to sleep at night. I saw the power of decisive action, because if I had wasted time in thinking about the matter, I could have missed out and I would have ended up somewhere different as a dissatisfied man.

I should like to say that I am a natural born soldier; this profession is what fits me well, and God knows that. I recall an incident where someone who knew me when I was in Chad said that if they took me out of the military, I would not have a job because this was the thing I knew how to do best. She reckoned that I was a natural-born soldier. She didn't know that I was also a teacher and a good farmer! Another person said that I was a soldier's soldier.

After two months the result of the entrance examination came out, and we were called for an interview. That was when I decided to tell my father about my decision to join the Army. I told him about all that had happened. In fact, the impression given to us was that we had already been admitted into the NDA. We thought we were just to go for training, not knowing that it was just an interview. So I met my father in the ministry, at hid place of work, because I was so eager to explain things to him that I couldn't wait for him to come home. He said, "Ah! This is a very good thing." He was so impressed with me. He said I should go along with my contemporaries, that I should go ahead and join the Army. I thanked him for his approval and blessings. I told him that what I needed most was his blessing. He gave me his advice, and that was how we went for the interview.

I was still in BOCOBS when this was happening. I missed classes for some time because of the NDA thing and some of my lecturers took notice of my absence in class because I was the punctual type. I was not in school for about a month, the whole of October 1981. I remember one of my lecturers who asked me where I went for such a long period. The lecturer was used to taking attendance. He knew that I was not attending class, so when I came back he took attendance and discovered I was around. He asked me to leave his class, since I had had the temerity to leave without permission.

When he finished, I followed him to his office to explain why I had been absent in class. By the time I had told him where I had gone, he had completely changed his attitude. He became so happy. This lecturer told me that military service was the best service one could do for one's country. He said it was a highly-respected profession all over the world. He was an Indian expatriate. He was very happy with me and promptly registered me back. I was taken aback by his action and sudden change of mind.

I said "Come! So, this military service is so special and highly respected!" That further encouraged me to go to the NDA to do my best as a cadet. In no distant time, they made me a Cadet Sergeant Major (CSM) at the NDA. Military service is one unique experience that everyone really needs to have a taste of, to experience it. I joined the Nigerian Army as a cadet in 1981, precisely on 3rd January 1981.

The NDA is more or less like any other university we have in Nigeria, but one thing that makes it different is that it has a Directorate of Military Training (DMT). The DMT is responsible for the day-to-day training of cadets in military related subjects and exercises and it is headed by a one-star Army officer. The Directorate has five Wings under it and each Wing is headed by a Chief Instructor (CI).

The first Wing is the Army Wing, which is headed by a CI with the rank of Major. It is the wing responsible for training and expounding everything about the Army to cadets in the NDA. Next to it is the Air Force Wing, which is headed by a CI with the rank of Group Captain. This wing is responsible for training and expounding everything about the Air Force to cadets who want to become Air Force officers.

As you know, the Nigerian Armed Forces is sub-divided in to three categories, so apart from the Army and the Air Force, we have the Navy. Those who want to become Naval officers are trained to become gallant naval officers in the Navy Wing, which is also headed by a CI with the rank of Navy Captain. We also have the Short Service Wing, which is responsible for the training of officers who have already acquired their degree or HND and are therefore classified as non-regulars. They are usually older than regular cadets and they don't go beyond nine months in the NDA.

The regular cadets spend up to four years in the Academy because they usually come in younger and stay for four years to acquire their degrees in the Academy. The academic programmes of the Academy are carefully tailored to meet the needs of the Nigerian Armed Forces within the context of standards required of Nigerian Universities[7]. The Short Service Wing is headed by a CI with the rank of Colonel. Last but not the least is the Training Support Wing (TSW) which is the responsible for the provision of technical support in training to all the four Wings. The TSW is headed by a CI who is an Army officer with the established rank of Colonel. The TSW has four departments under

7. This assertion was made by the Academy on its website

THE LEGEND OF BURATAI - VOLUME II

it which are as follows: Weapons Training, Signal, Physical Training and the Engineering Training Team. Each of these departments is headed by a Major.

Lastly, there is what is known as the Demo Battalion, and it is headed by a Lieutenant Colonel. Demo Battalion is responsible for the provision of practical demonstration in all aspects of military training activities and support during training exercises.

After my commissioning, I got admission into the University of Maiduguri to study history. That was in 1986, but I wasn't able to make it. I had to differ it to 1987 because I couldn't get permission to proceed with the studies in 1986. I was finally released in 1987 to proceed with my studies. As I was preparing to start the academic programme, I discussed with my friends and colleagues in the office about my intention to pursue a degree programme. I told them that I was going to the University of Maiduguri to study for a degree in history and to my surprise they were all shocked.

They asked what I was going there to do. In fact, they said that to go there would be a waste of time. They said that I would face economic challenges if I went, and advised that I should stay back in my unit and make money. I still don't understand what they meant by 'staying in my unit to make money'. I was taken aback. Instead of encouraging me to study, they were saying it is not good to study. I just wanted to improve myself. I ignored them and their advice. I made up my mind to do what I thought was right and best for my life. I said that the money could wait. Whatever happened, I had to go and get this degree.

That was how I went to the University of Maiduguri. I got my first degree and second degree through diligence and hard work. Same with the Masters in Philosophy I obtained from the Bangladeshi University of Professionals which is partially affiliated to the National Defence College of Bangladesh (NDE) The NDE is an institution dedicated to the development

and security studies as it affects the developing world. It provides training to select senior military and civil officers from on national and international security related fields as well as to impart training to mid ranking military officers of Bangladesh on war studies. It was established following the decision of the Government of the People's Republic of Bangladesh in December 1996 and the first National Defence Course commenced on 10 January 1999 in the premises of Defence Services Command and Staff College, Mirpur. A three-member

British Defence Advisory Team assisted in structuring the first National Defence Course. The Course was designed to make the senior military and civil services officers aware of the nitty-gritty of national security in broader perspectives, the opportunities and threats of geo-politics and its related strategic imperatives. Part of the course work and the assessment was on my defence studies and having met all the criteria I was awarded Masters in Philosophy (M.Phil.) in Security Studies because NDE is affiliated to the University of the Professionals, Dhaka. Today, I am by the grace of God a member of NDE's Hall of Fame to be precise, fourth on the list.

So, education is a good thing, and it is fundamental to achieving success in life. Once you are educated you will have an open mind and a broader, more global perspective to things which will eventually make you a better person. This has greatly helped me in my career as an officer.

Throughout my career, anywhere I served, especially those staff appointments that I held, my bosses never allowed me to leave because of the kind of output I gave to them. That is why I spent up to four years in some places. I am grateful for the opportunity given to me by President Buhari to serve as COAS, but as you see, my output had made him retain me for more than four years. I was in Army Headquarters as a staff officer and as a Colonel. That also helped me in the Staff College. You know, I got my Masters before I went to the college as a student as well as a member of the Directing Staff, and then went back as a Director at the Department of Warfare in the Staff College. I thank God for giving me the capacity and the opportunity to educate myself.

❧ LESSON ❧

Don't get carried away with the obsession with becoming a general. Instead focus on whatever assignment is assigned to you at the moment and try to do it well. If you do it well, you will get satisfied, master what you did and make the universe know that you are ready for greater assignments. The universe will arrange to see you get greater assignments which means greater responsibility which is synonymous with greater leadership. That is generalship. Do the small assignments very well if you want to be entrusted with greater assignments.

HALL OF FAME OF THE NATIONAL DEFENCE COLLEGE, BANGLADESH

General Moeen U Ahmed.

is a former Bangladesh Army General and the 12th Chief of Army Staff of the Bangladesh Army from 15 June 2005 to 15 June 2009 with last one-year extension during the caretaker government led by Fakhruddin Ahmed. He has worked in Bangladesh High Commission in Islamabad, Pakistan as a Defence Attaché in the rank of Brigadier, and prior to that he served as a UN Peacekeeper in United Nations Assistance Mission for Rwanda as a Colonel in 1995.

Years of service: 1975 to 2009

General Mohammed Abdul Mubeen.

is a Bangladeshi General who served as the 13th Chief of Staff of the Bangladesh Army. Prior to his service as Chief of Army Staff, Mubeen served as Principal staff officer of the Armed Forces Division.

Years of service: 16 June 2009 – 25 June 2012

General Bilal Shafiul Huq.

is a Bangladesh army general and the chief of staff of the Bangladesh Army, in office from 25 June 2015 to 25 June 2018. Before his tenure as chief of staff he served as the Principal Staff Officer of Prime Minister's Office of the Armed Forces Division.

Years of service: 1978 to 2018

Lt. General Tukur Yusufu Buratai:

is the 24th Chief of Staff of the Nigerian Army. He was commissioned in 1983 and was appointed COAS in June 2015.

Years of service: 1983 to present

Rear Admiral Shah Iqbal Mujtaba.

commanded various kinds of ships and establishments. He performed as Director of Naval Operations (DNO), Director of Naval Plans (DNP) and Director of Naval Intelligence (DNI) at Naval Headquarters.

Years of service: 1970 to 2005

Rear Admiral M Hasan Ali Khan, NDC, PSC, BN (died February 19, 2013) was Chief of Staff of the Bangladesh Navy between 2005 and 2007. He was preceded by Rear Admiral Shah Iqbal Mujtaba ndc, psc, BN and succeeded by Vice Admiral Sarwar Jahan Nizam ndu, psc, BN.

Years of service: 1972 to 2007

Vice Admiral Zahir Uddin Ahmed (ND), NBP, BCGM, ndc, psc. (born 1957) was Chief of Naval Staff of the Bangladesh Navy. He was preceded by Vice Admiral Sarwar Jahan Nizam ndu, psc, BN and succeeded by Vice Admiral M Farid Habib, ndc, psc.

Years of service: 1979 to 2013

Admiral M Farid Habib (ND), NBP, OSP, BCGM, NDC, PSC (born 1959) was the 14th Chief of Staff of the Bangladesh Navy. He is the first ever four-star Admiral in the history of Bangladesh Navy

Years of service: 1979 – January 27, 2016

DESTINY AND THE ARMY

Vice Admiral Sarwar Jahan Nizam. ndu, psc, BN (born 1952) is the first ever Vice-Admiral and Ex-Chief of Staff for the Bangladesh Navy. He is preceded by Rear Admiral M Hasan Ali Khan ndc, psc, BN and succeeded by Vice Admiral Zahir Uddin Ahmed (ND) ndc, psc, BN.
Years of service: 1973 to 2009

Admiral Aurangzeb Chowdhury NBP, OSP, BCGM, PCGM, BCGMS, ndc, psc, BN, is a four-star Admiral of Bangladesh and the current Chief of Staff of the Bangladesh Navy. Previously, he held the post of Director General of the Bangladesh Coast Guard.
Years of service: 10 December 1980 – present

Air Marshal (rtd.) Muhammad Enamul Bari is a former Bangladesh Air Force officer whose last assignment before retiring was the 13th Chief of Air Staff of Bangladesh Air Force. He retired on June 12, 2015 after over 30 years of service
Years of Service: 13 June 2012 to 12 June 2015

Air Chief Marshal Abu Esrar, BBP, NDC, ACSC is the current and 14th Chief of the Air Staff of the Bangladesh Air Force. He took over as the chief on 12 June 2015 from Air Marshal Enamul Bari. He is the first four-star air officer (Air Chief Marshal) of Bangladesh. He was promoted to ACM on 16 January 2016.

Years of service: 1 February 1981 - 11 June 2018

At the National Defence College Bangladesh 2008 (2nd Row, First from left)

Cadets in training

National Defence College Bangladesh. 2010 reunion. I am second from left in suit above and agbada below.

National Defence College Bangladesh. 2010 reunion.

At the Taj Mahal, India

Lt Gen Buratai at a BBC Hard Talk Interview with Steven Sackur in 2017
© BBC Hard Talk

"To live at all is miracle enough."

Mervyn Peake

CHAPTER FIVE

❖ ❖ ❖

THE MIRACULOUS ESCAPE

When I was a child growing up, I did a lot of observation and not so much talking. I am the kind of person who likes to observe my surroundings and people as well. I was always alert as a boy and sometimes reckless to a fault. Although I could be indecisive as a boy, whenever I made up my mind to do something, I never turned back, no matter what the risks. Even as a boy, I was not accustomed to fear.

The first mishap in my life happened when I was just eight years old, in 1968 in the Lamisula Ward of Maiduguri. There used to be a pond at Lamisula at that time and boys of my age and above usually went there to swim and do the boyish things boys everywhere do to amuse themselves. My older brother was a good swimmer and he liked to go to the pond to swim every now and then. I used to accompany him whenever he went, but I didn't swim at all. Instead I stayed aloof or sat down on the edge of the pond and watched how the other boys and my brother swam and amused themselves in the pond. I think I was somewhat suspicious of the pond at that time.

Stories abound of how this pond led to the deaths of many children in the neighbourhood. Besides, I am the kind of person who can be shy and reserved in the crowd. I have never been a coward in my life, but I know that I have been reserved and an introvert.

On this particular day in 1968 I decided to take the initiative of swimming on my own. I didn't consult anybody. I just watched how the other boys were amusing themselves and decided that I must jump into the pond and amuse myself as well. So, in the twinkling of an eye, I was in the water. But something strange happened that day. Immediately upon jumping into the pond, I sank beneath the water and stayed there like a stone. I didn't know how to swim at that time and my brother didn't even know that I had jumped in. Like Prophet Jonah, I stayed there in the water, but not for three days and nights!

Even as I reflected on what to do I said to myself in a low voice, "You will make it out of this water". I was not scared or worried beneath the water. I can't recall the exact time I spent there, but I stayed there for a considerable length of time.

One of the big boys, by the name of Adamu, knew how to swim very well. His father used to be a fisherman in the Lake Chad River and he was born in Baga town, the prosperous town sacked by Boko Haram insurgents before I assumed the position of Chief of Army Staff. The town is situated near the river and most people who settled in Baga settled there because of the thriving fishing trade. Everyone you see in Baga is directly or indirectly linked to the fishery business. He or she is either there to catch fish or provide services and goods to those who catch fish in the river. Adamu learnt how to swim in Baga.

For reasons that neither Adamu nor I can comprehend, Adamu swam in my direction.

"Kai! Akwai mutum anan fa," he said when his leg touched my body— "What! There is someone here," in Hausa.

Adamu was a strong boy. He wasted no time and followed his instinct. He just dived under the water again, grabbed my body and raised me up. He brought me to the edge of the pond and put me down. All the other boys stopped what they were doing and gathered around me. My eyes were closed and I appeared not to be breathing. Some of the boys thought I had drowned. Adamu, my brother Ibrahim and the other boys decided to press my stomach and chest in the hope that I would vomit the water out. Nothing came out of my mouth, because I hadn't drunk any water while I was in the pond.

What happened next was a miracle. I just opened my eyes and sat upright. The whole thing turned into frenzy. No one knew how I had survived that incident. It was a shock to everyone in the neighbourhood. I think my father began to take a special interest in me that very day. Something in him told him that I was not an ordinary child; that the hand of the Almighty was with me. What he didn't know, because I didn't tell anyone, was that a fierce battle had taken place between the forces of darkness and those of light over my survival. The forces of darkness wanted to kill me, but God's angels protected me and saved me. I was not destined to die at that tender age. That was not the plan of the Almighty. It was after that experience that I first became conscious of what death is. It was also that experience that taught me how important it is to rescue people from danger.

I had a wonderful childhood, enriched by my family and friends. Most of these childhood friends are still alive and we do meet from time to time. I remember how we used to go to the bush to hunt for birds in Buratai with Ibrahim Ya Musa Bam, who is now based in Kaduna. I like hunting because it helps me to connect with nature.

I was six years old and was watching as my brother and his friends swam in the pond. I would later jump into the pond myself.

❧ LESSON ❧

If God has earmarked you for something, no mortal or any negative power can change His plan. However, that doesn't mean you will have an easy ride in your life's journey to reach and fulfil your destiny. Furthermore, it is good to enjoy life and amuse yourself. Play hard and also work hard.

The Commander must at constant pains keep his troops abreast of all the latest tactical experience and developments, and must insist on their practical application. He must see to it that his subordinates are trained in accordance with the latest requirements. The best form of welfare for the troops is first class training, for this saves unnecessary casualties.

General Erwin Rommel

CHAPTER SIX

❖ ❖ ❖

Generalship

I should like to say that my destiny and that of President Buhari are closely intertwined. For example, he was born in 1942, the same year that my father enlisted in the Army. Secondly, we are both connected to the name Yusuf. Yusuf is the same name as Joseph and the name was first used by one of the sons of Jacob, who is also known as Yakub in the Arabic tongue. The name of the president's oldest son is Yusuf and my father's name is Yusufu.

I am also certain that the President influenced me to a great extent. Whenever I am asked about those people who influenced me, I try to avoid talking of a specific role model. I would say that many people made a good impression on me because of their exemplary lives. These individuals were very firm, focused, diligent and patriotic to the nation, but that of the president (Major General Muhammadu Buhari in 1984) was exceptional.

President Buhari (middle) Governor Nasir el-Rufai (left) and myself (right) admiring an enlarge picture of the President with some of his comrades when he was serving in the Army. The event was the COAS Conference, 2019 that was held in Kaduna.

For example, President Buhari came into the limelight when he became the Head of State in 1984. It happened that this was the same year, or almost the same period, that I graduated from the Nigerian Defence Academy as a Second Lieutenant. When he came in 1983, we had not even reported to our various units because we had just left the Academy in December. Before we reported to our units, he came as the Head of State. Everybody knows who Mr President is and what he stands for. He is upright, a gentleman, a disciplinarian, diligent, focused, and highly patriotic. These are the values that can make one say "yes, I have a good leader to emulate." Everybody loves him for his uprightness, for his character, for his attitude.

I am a historian, so I take time to read about the leadership style and qualities of many people. As

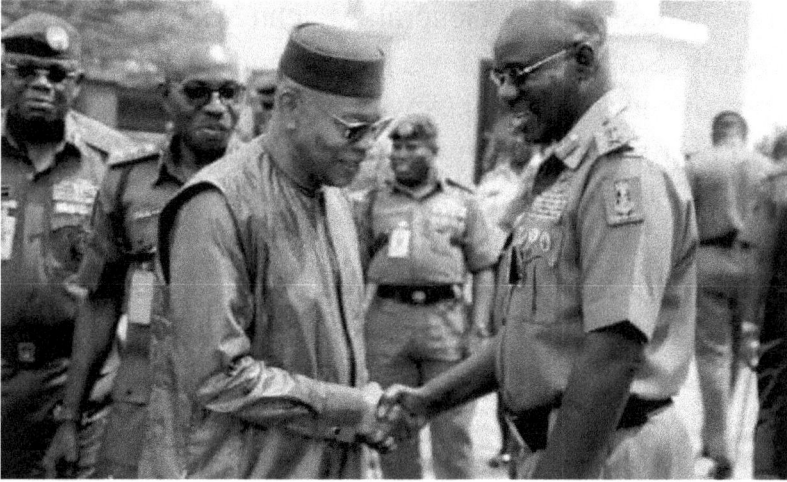

The UN Special Representative for West Africa and the Sahel, Dr. Mohamed Ibn Chambas, applauded the Nigerian Army during his visit to the Army Headquarters in Abuja.

Chambas said, "One area of interest is the ongoing efforts to checkmate Boko Haram and stop its spread because of its affiliation to international terror groups. That is why it is incumbent on us all that we must see the fight againstBoko Haram as a fight against international terrorism.

students of history, we read about the President's perspective and style of leadership. What I like most about the President is his persistence and his ability to pursue whatever he sets as a goal until he gets it. He follows it through to the end until he succeeds. He doesn't make too much noise about anything to impress anybody. I would say that I have come across several other commanders who have proved to be upright, hardworking, committed and patriotic. I know we have worked with now Retired Major General Zidon, who was the Commanding Officer 26 Guards Brigade. We have also worked with now retired Brigadier General Abu Ahmadu, and with now retired Major General Chris Abutu Garba in the United Nations.

I remember when General Abacha was the Chief of Army Staff; he was very firm and resolute. His responsiveness to troops' welfare was such that he didn't play with it. There was a time when our barracks in Elele were destroyed by a storm, but within a week or so we were able to fix them. Great soldiers like George Patton, Montgomery, Rommel and a host of others also made a great impression on my career. I read about them. When I was appointed as COAS, all these have come to bear as character models. The appointment is not for you, the officer, but for the troops and their families, and anything that affects them must be of interest to you. This is because you can't be a chief without the troops.

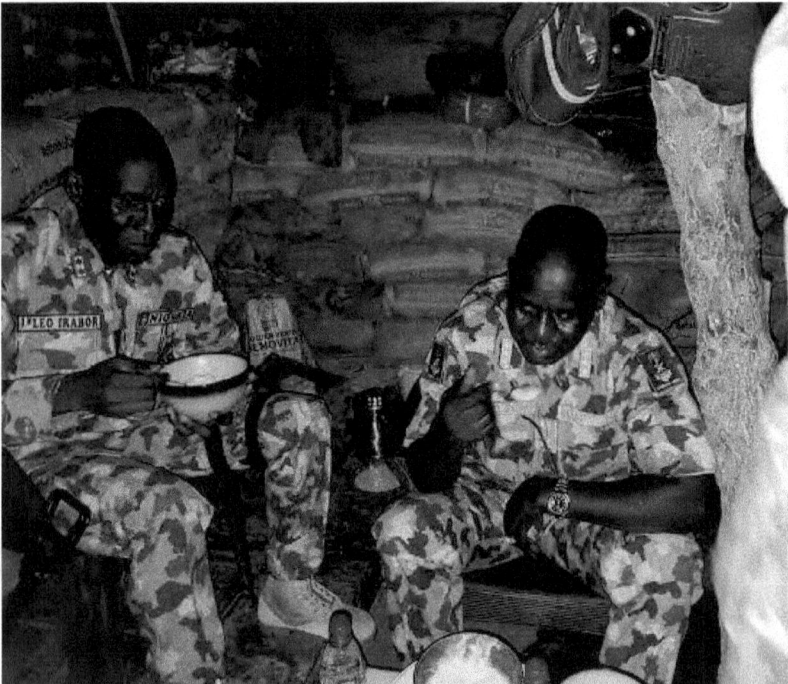

Major General LEO irabor and myself in the bush with troops of Operation Lafiya Dole. In this picture, we were eating inside a tent. General Irabor is among the outstanding theatre commanders who led Operation Lafiya Dole.

Major General LEO irabor and myself in the bush with troops of Operation Lafiya Dole. In this picture, we were eating inside a tent. General Irabor is among the outstanding theatre commanders who led Operation Lafiya Dole.

When I took over as Chief of Army Staff, I said to myself that this assignment was not about sitting down in the office. "I can't sit down in the office when my soldiers are in the theatre of operations," I had said to myself. The soldiers must see me as their leader and I must make them understand that they are fighting for a good cause." I quickly moved to the field to go and do what I have been trained to do as an infantry general.

One big advantage is that I hail from the north-east region, Borno to be precise. At least I have a fair idea of the terrain. I gathered some vital intelligence about the movements of the terrorists and their strategies. I made up my mind to visit the theatre of operations in the north-east to interact with the troops and know what the challenges were. I knew that we must realign the troops on the ground and give them direction.

I addressed the troops and made them feel indestructible. I made them understand that theirs was a higher calling and that the whole country was counting on them. "The Nigerian Army I used to know is a strong force made up of warriors," I said. "The Nigerian Army has proved that we are warriors in Liberia and Sierra Leone. I expect exceptional gallantry as we begin to march into the camp of the enemy to reclaim every piece of earth that belongs to our Fatherland." I ate, prayed, slept and partied with them.

After going round the theatre of operations to see things for myself, I realised out that most of the challenges were coming from some parts of Yobe,

Saluting the Commander-in-Chief of the Armed
Forces at the State House, Abuja.

As a Brigadier General standing obediently behind the then Chief of Army Staff, Lt. General Abdurahman Danbazzau in 2009.

most parts of Borno and northern Adamawa. When the terrorists were flushed out from Maiduguri Metropolis, they moved to Sambisa, and it was from there that they started moving into northern Adamawa, Michika, Mubi and other areas. I discovered that no attention was placed on other places apart from Maiduguri. So I said no, we have to change our approach.

The focus should not just be the protection of Maiduguri to the detriment of other places, because once they dominate the periphery, they will convert everybody into their own group and swell up their ranks. Then those that remain in the city centre will become vulnerable. So I said I would not start from Maiduguri, to which everybody was paying much attention. Instead, I started from Damaturu.

President Buhari decorating me with my new rank of
Lieutenant General in 2015

Explaining an important aspect of the warfare to my
Commander-in-Chief in Maiduguri

AFSSC
Jaji,2000.Exercise, Haske Biyu.

My first point of call as soon as I got appointed as Chief of Army Staff was Damaturu, because I knew it was the right place for us to plan the engagement and extinction of the enemy. I could remember that I celebrated the sallah (celebrations) with the troops and this whole thing happened in July 2015. I gave new directives for the creation of a new brigade because the 3 Division was always shuttling between Yola, Damaturu and Jos, and hardly stayed for three days in Damaturu, where they ought to be. So I gave a new directive that the 3 Division should be moved down to Damaturu and a new brigade should be created around Benisheikh.

The 27 brigade was also created in Buni Yadi town. If you recall, Buni Yadi was the town where the insurgents displayed to the whole world that they were barbarians who had no regard for the lives of innocent children.

As a cadet in the NDA. Here I was returning from lectures with my friend Officer Cadet O Uzoma.

It was in Buni Yadi that fifty-six innocent boys were slaughtered in an institution of learning belonging to the federal government—the Federal Government College. The massacre of these innocent children still gives me nightmares whenever I remember the sad event. They were massacred for no just reason; their offence was that they were in school to receive an education, something the insurgents regarded as *haram* or forbidden.

Is it not strange? Education was now *haram*! The insurgents became notorious through utterances like "Boko Haram," which in the English tongue can be loosely translated to "Western-oriented education is forbidden by God." I placed a Brigade there! If you look at the modus operandi of the Boko Haram insurgency during 2013, 2014 and 2015, apart from northern Borno which they dominated by December 2015 after they drove the Multi-National Joint Task Force, you will discover that they launched every attack from Buni Yadi. In fact, they attacked Buni Yadi several times. The last one, which made everybody abandon the town, was when they attacked the Federal Government College there. They have also ransacked and occupied Gamborun-Ngala and Dikwa. It was only Mafa that had troops.

I knew that we had to restrict their movement or at least make it difficult for them to move around to attack innocent Nigerians. That was why I considered it foremost and imperative for a brigade to be taken to Buni Yadi and then put the Division in Damaturu. By the time we moved to Buni Yadi, we had effectively blocked them. We made sure they could not come across and go to Bauchi and Gombe and possibly Jos. That was their route. That is why they insisted on clearing and taking over Buni Yadi. They followed the rail line through to Gulani and we blocked them in that axis. Subsequently, we created a brigade in Benisheikh which was stationed in Alagarno. It was after that that I ordered the capture of Dikwa and the whole thing was done within a week.

The troops were highly mobilized and we made them observe rigorous operational readiness exercises. Within one week, General Adeosun, the then GOC, mobilized his troops, routed the insurgents, unleashed pandemonium on their heads through the use of heavy fire and bombardment and captured Dikwa. They discovered so many things there — an improvised explosive device-making factory, specialised communication gadgets, and so on. After a month we consolidated and proceeded to villages around that area to clear the remnants of the insurgents that were hiding there.

We wasted no time in drawing up a plan to exterminate the insurgents in Gamboru-Ngala and reclaim it back so that constituted authority could be re-established. It took the troops almost a month and some days, because the road was bad and there were landmines littered everywhere by the insurgents. In fact, some of our troops were affected by mines in the operation.

It took the troops almost three months to capture Gamboru-Ngala. The insurgents received a lot of foreign support from neighbouring countries. Some of their fighters looked like our neighbours, and most don't understand Hausa or Kanuri. In Gamboru-Ngala, the troops showed the insurgents that the Army was more than their match. The insurgents were completely neutralized. A large number of them were killed, but a few of them escaped through Fotokol to Cameroun. No soldier was killed, but a few were wounded.

It was within the first week of my assumption that we went to Konduga and changed the name of the operation from *Zaman Lafiya* to *Lafiya Dole*. *Zaman Lafiya* is a Hausa phrase which means peaceful existence or living in peace and harmony. I suggested that it should be changed because it didn't have the kind of force I wanted it to carry. *Lafiya Dole* is a Hausa phrase which means peaceful coexistence or that living in peace and harmony is compulsory and not negotiable.

We want to enforce peace by engaging the enemies of peace and extinguishing them altogether. That doesn't mean I subscribe to the tenets or ideology of Robert Taber, who said that the only way to deal with the insurgents was to kill them and turn their hideouts into a desert—no. We gave them the opportunity to surrender to the government or else be exterminated.

Lafiya Dole was meant to change the psyche of the troops and the locales, to make them understand that we mean business. This was just to subconsciously change their minds. The choice of Hausa words was because Hausa is the lingua franca of the area and we wanted to contextualize the operation and make the locals see it as a collective effort. We were not begging for peace but demanding that peace be maintained, and we were

Leading a push-up exercise. I believe that regular exercise is needed to keep soldiers fit for operations.

serious about it. Even though we were soldiers, we had no pleasure in war, because we know that lives will be wasted, but war is necessary when it becomes the only means of enforcing peace.

The main objective of Operation Lafiya Dole is to defeat Boko Haram insurgents, rescue all persons abducted, including the Chibok girls, and equally to ensure the restoration of civil authority in those areas that were hitherto captured by the Boko Haram terrorists. This will also lead to the provision of security and facilitation of movements of national and international NGOs and government agencies to provide relief materials to Internally Displaced Persons (IDPs). Basically, this was the concept behind Operation Lafiya Dole.

Something had bothered me when I served as Commander of the Multi-National Joint Task Force

(MNJTF) in Ndjamena, the capital of Chad. When Mr President came in as the President and Commander in Chief, he did not mince his words on fighting and defeating the Boko Haram insurgency. A pledge of 100 million US dollars was made before he was sworn in. When he took over as President, he immediately fulfilled that pledge to the Multi-National Joint Task Force. This is what is sustaining it. This has been very useful, and it has helped in the war against terror and in supporting other countries. So this is a commitment by Mr President which he has fulfilled.

The MNJTF comprises Nigeria, Chad, Cameroun, Niger and Benin Republic. The leaders of these countries had come up with a plan to give the MNJTF more teeth in 2015, although discussions started much earlier, in 2013 and then in 2014. The countries pledged to provide troops and also to block Boko Haram infiltration into their countries. Sector One of the MNJTF was stationed in Cameroun, while Sector Two was Chad, but Sector Two's troops were not to be stationed in Chadian territory but on Nigerian territory. That meant Chadian troops would be deployed in Nigeria. Then Sector 3 would be supplied from Nigeria at Baga.

I wasn't comfortable with this arrangement because to my mind it undermined our national sovereignty. I was worried about the issue of Chadian troops deployed on Nigerian territory. The issue of sovereignty is fundamental. When I saw the white paper on this deployment, it had already been approved. I was about to implement these deployments because they were orders that needed to be obeyed. I had not yet been appointed Chief of Army Staff, so I couldn't change it as the Force Commander; I had no option but to implement the deployments. But in my mind I was not comfortable and I said, if given the chance, that I would make sure it didn't happen.

So we were in the process of implementation and I went to the French Operation Base in Ndjemena, called Operation Barkhane. It consists of troops from France who were supporting Mali, Chad and Cameroun in the fight against terrorism, generally. I think they had some kind of bilateral or multi-lateral agreement for them to operate. They were supporting them with combat operation, ISR (intelligence, surveillance and reconnaissance) as well as logistics and medical supplies.

In Port Harcourt, with former GOC 6 Div (now Commandant NDA), Major General Jamil Sarham and other officers.

Directly interfacing with officers and men of Operation Lafiya Dole in Maiduguri to ascertain how they are coping with a view to addressing some of their immediate problems in 2018.

I met the Commander of Operation Barkhane at his headquarters and while we were talking, he asked what would be my priority if I were to embark on the operation. Which area would I clear first? Would it be the northern front, the central front or the southern front? I told him that I would start from the central front— that was the first area I would clear before I would go to the northern front. He was surprised to hear that. They had the ISR, and they had been monitoring all the activities of the terrorists in those areas. They knew the strength of the terrorists in those areas. He asked me why, and I told him that first of all, I must separate the two groups, and for that to happen, I would have to attack the centre so that the north and the south could not cross to meet each other. I don't know whether he was convinced with my assessment or not, but that was my own idea.

Luckily, after a month or so, my appointment came as the Chief of Army Staff, Nigerian Army. I saw it as an opportunity for me to really block the issue of infiltration of Nigeria by foreign troops. So, I quickly directed that we take over Dikwa up to the Cameroonian border. Much to the dismay of many, within a few months, we had taken over Gamborun-Ngala. So that sealed the earlier plan for Chadian troops to come into Nigerian territory.

When they eventually asked me if they could come into the country as earlier agreed, I declined to consent. I said, "Come to where?" The new Multi-National Joint Task Force Commander was asking whether the Chadian troops could come in and take over the operation. I said, "No, I cannot do that, I cannot allow them to come into our Fatherland. We are going to take care of those areas which the insurgents are controlling. General, we are more than able to reclaim those territories, so tell the Chadian forces to stand down." And that was the end of the matter. That was how we prevented the infiltration of foreign troops into this country.

You see, terrorism as rightly portrayed by General Powell in his autobiography has now become a global challenge. When this plague was devastating places like Somalia, Iraq, Afghanistan and Mali, we had the erroneous impression that it would never come into this part of the world. And the issue of suicide bombing was remote, in our imagination. We sat down and carried on with our lives as if we were not interconnected with the rest of the world, without planning against it, without taking appropriate measures to prevent any infiltration. Unfortunately, it has now come into our homes, and it has taken a very serious toll on the country, especially the north-eastern part, but the whole country has been affected. The fallout of the clash of these herdsmen-farmers, banditry and cattle rustling, was all part of the Boko Haram insurgency.

We intensified a number of actions that helped our troops to get to the terrorists before they ran out of their hideouts or caused havoc. But to totally wipe out Boko Haram, we require the support of everybody. They live among us and are everywhere, and we require very good intelligence to fish them out. The most important thing is to prevent them from having the capacity to launch attacks on innocent individuals and on our troops' location.

For us to deal with insurgency we must formulate and adopt a comprehensive approach to development, because you never know from which angle the security challenge will come from. If it is food security, we must tackle it. If it is the challenge of education, we must tackle it, otherwise it is this aspect that miscreants and some misguided elements will exploit to cause serious security breaches in the country, as we have seen in the case of Boko Haram.

Things had got really bad when I came in as Chief of Army Staff. There were several challenges, and we tried to address them. These challenges require serious attention, but we tried to do our best to mitigate them. However, that doesn't mean we don't have challenges here on our own side. We still do, especially in the

I hosted officers and men of Operation Lafiya Dole to a dinner in Maiduguri so that I could directly interface with them in order to know what are their challenges in the theatre.

area of funding, because every war is capital intensive. The most important thing is that whatever challenges we have, we seek ways to address them quickly. For example, the morale of the troops was low when we came on board. To me this was unacceptable, because there is no way a demoralised soldier can fight and give you results.

I didn't just sit in Abuja or the Headquarters of the Theatre Command; I went to meet with the troops in the field. One of my cardinal principles in warfare is the visitation of troops by their commanders. This is why I made it a habit to see them every now and then. When I could not make it, I delegated someone to represent me, but in most cases I went myself. Visitation is always effective in revitalising the mind-set of troops. You cannot deploy men to somewhere in the jungle and then leave them to be on their own without coming in to listen to their challenges.

Secondly, we try to see that our troops are trained at all times. Any unit or formation or group of soldiers that is coming into the theatre of operation has to be retrained so that they can be fit for the onerous assignment that brought them there. Training is very important to the Army and no one can reach a level where he or she will say that training is no longer needed. The training is an ongoing process which we intend to sustain. We were able to establish the Special Forces School in Buni Yadi and it is doing very well. So this aspect of the challenge of training we are able to address, and we will continue to improve on it.

We also discovered that the issue of equipment and military hardware was one of the reasons the troops were demoralised and the insurgents were recording some success in 2014. We wasted no time in addressing this issue. After having procured some equipment, we were also able to repair a lot of our fighting vehicles and inject them into the operation. We were able to send large numbers of troop-carrying vehicles, and indeed some operational vehicles, into the theatre. That also changed the situation. We were able to look at the logistical challenges and improvised a workable solution. We made sure that arms and ammunition were provided regularly and in the required quantity. We also ensured that the soldiers' basic needs in terms of comfort, uniforms and protective gear were provided. Hitherto, all of these things had been in very short supply. As for medical care and emergency services, we were able to look into that and quickly revitalise the unit, because I knew that was vital to our operations.

We provided more ambulances, more drugs and an effective system of casualty evacuation.

Another issue that I didn't mess with was the salaries of the troops. To me their pay and allowances were issues I consider sacred, so we ensured that they were paid regularly and when due. No general worth his salt will send his troops to the front line and then deprive them of their wages. Every soldier deserves to receive his pay immediately after the usual thirty days. No one should delay payment, no matter what, because of all the citizens of a country, it is the soldier who is out there protecting it with his life. If a country can afford to be lackadaisical over the wages of its troops, that country will collapse before long.

We didn't stop at the prompt and regular payment of soldier's wages; we also tried to make their families comfortable by making sure they were well catered for. We embarked on renovating the troops' accommodation. We constructed new buildings where there were shortages, and this we shall continue to do. We will continue to improve on that.

With regard to what I call operational challenges, I think we are still trying to do our best by devising ways to use what we have on the ground to get value. When I say operational challenges, I mean the kind of challenges troops encounter in fighting insurgents. For example, the issue of landmass is something else, because the landmass of the north-east is very large. The North-Eastern region is the size of France and Italy together, or Togo, Benin and Equatorial Guinea put together.

Dignitaries at the presentation of The Legend of Buratai Volume One in Port Harcourt. Standing in the middle is HRM King Diette Spiff, the Amanyanabo of Twon Brass Kingdom, representative of the GOC, Major General Penap and other senior Army officers and traditional chiefs.

There are not enough boots to cover every square metre of the land with troops. We have other areas in the country that require the attention and presence of troops, so there is no way we can put them all into the North-East. Space allows insurgents to decide where and when to fight. The army cannot be everywhere at once without spreading our forces too thinly and inviting attack from the insurgents at our weakest points. we have done a lot to ensure that we deploy more troops since I became Chief of Army Staff. We have been able to move across the entire north-east because of the availability of mobility equipment.

The issue of insurgency and terrorism is not something that is restricted to a particular religion. Religious fundamentalism is not always negative, but there are many instances where it too easily led to extremism and violence. The case of Myanmar is a typical example of how Buddhism, a religion considered to be peaceful, turned out to be violent. In fact, what is interesting about this case is that those being persecuted and killed by the Buddhists are Muslims—the Rohingya Muslims. Hitherto, some people reckoned Muslims to be violent, so they labelled all Muslims as terrorists because of the erroneous actions of groups like al Shabab, Ansaru and Boko Haram. This is a misunderstanding.

So I don't believe it is right to label one particular religion as violent, because all the revealed religions teach peace and love. The problem with religion happens when man hijacks it to achieve a political agenda, as in the case of the Boko Haram insurgents and the Lord's Resistance Army (LRA). The LRA is a special example, because it is today the longest serving insurgency group in Africa. It was started in 1987 by a man known as Joseph Kony, who said he wanted to rule northern Uganda with the Ten Commandments. The LRA is an international nuisance because of the tacit support it received over the years from Khartoum, which wanted to deal with Uganda for the support it gave to the Sudanese People's Liberation Army (SPLA). Just as the LRA is operating in South Sudan, Democratic Republic of Congo and Uganda, that's how Boko Haram is also operating in Nigeria, Cameroon and Chad. The LRA is thriving because of the logistics and arms it has been receiving from foreign governments. Someone is always available to fan the embers of crisis in Africa. In Mali, the Fulani and the Dogon people are now fighting each other after co-existing as brothers for years.

As a Company Commander of Support Company of 82 Battalion Operations Bakassi Peninsula) in 1998. Sitting next to him is the boat operator, Sargent Christopher Habila.

Most people don't know that this is complex warfare because of the support the insurgents and terrorists are receiving from unknown quarters. They had littered access routes to their hideouts with mines, and this is affecting the mobility or movement of troops. We have to move very cautiously and very slowly in some parts of the theatre.

Our troops have been killed and some wounded as a result of attacks where the insurgents planted IEDs on the roads, so we suffered casualties to vehicles and to our personnel and indeed civilians too. This is very unfortunate, but we have taken steps to procure some equipment to de-mine the theatre of operations. The hand-held equipment had been very useful in helping us to locate mines and disarm them. There are always limitations on the use of this equipment. Nevertheless, we will continue to do our best to ensure that we make our roads safe, and we would increase our vigilance, because it is important.

We are really happy; things are getting stabilised in the north-east. Except for some parts of Borno; Yobe and Adamawa are now totally stabilised. But that is not to say that we have come to the end. Terrorism, as we can see, is going to be an open-ended phenomenon, in the sense that if we allow these insurgents a little space, if there is even one month without any action they will come back. This means that no one should rest in his efforts, at Federal, State or local government level or on an individual basis. The security agencies don't have any time to rest, as they must be on top of the situation at all times. I tell you, give these criminals six months and they will come back. Time is the most important element required for the successful conclusion of an insurgent and terrorist campaign as it is a commodity that can be exchanged to make up for other weaknesses. With sufficient time, an insurgent group can organise itself, sap the resolve of its adversary, and build a conventional force capable of seizing control of the state. So on our part we are not going to rest in our effort. We will continue with our operations, clearance operation and surveillance and we will continue to show our presence.

When I took over as Chief of Army Staff I gave out my marching orders, which articulated my vision on how I envisaged the army to be. I made it clear that my vision was "to have a professionally responsive Nigerian Army in the discharge of its constitutional roles." This, I can tell you, has now been achieved. We have never had it so good in the Army, because of the amount of training that we have sent officers and soldiers to receive within and outside the country.

We organised numerous training exercises as well as the various seminars that were yielding the desired result. We renovated so many barracks and built new accommodations. We provided the best medical care for our wounded troops. We also created certain institutions —the new building of the Directorate of Military Intelligence, The Cyber Warfare Command Centre, the Army Aviation, newly established command schools, new army formations, Command Engineering Depot (Vehicle) plant in Kaduna, Nigerian Army University in Biu and the Nigerian Army Resource Centre (NARC).

The NARC is one key institution that was initiated and developed by our leadership. It is a think-tank for the Nigerian Army which we hope in time will grow to provide advice and also some papers for national issues. I think one can be highly satisfied with what I have achieved so far. I pray that Almighty Allah protects me from all malice, because some people are just out to malign others or get others smeared, simply because of envy. These are things that are bound to happen whenever one is occupying an important position in life. As Chief of Army Staff, I know that I have to contend with different characters and attitudes and that's okay. But in the end, the truth will always prevail.

The NARC is one key institution that was initiated and developed by our leadership. It is a think-tank for the Nigerian Army which we hope in time will grow to a national think-tank. I am highly satisfied with what I have achieved so far. I pray that Almighty Allah continues to protect me to contribute to the Nigerian Army, even after retirement.

∾ LESSON ∾

Don't get carried away with the obsession to become a general. Instead focus on whatever assignment is assigned to you at the moment and try to do it well. If you do it well, you will achieve satisfaction, master what you did and make the universe know that you are ready for more. The universe will arrange to see you get greater assignments, which means greater responsibility, which is synonymous with greater leadership. That is generalship. If you want to be entrusted with greater assignments, do the small assignments very well.

"Always do everything you ask of those you command."

General George S. Patton, US Army

CHAPTER seven

❖ ❖ ❖

THE SECRETS OF LEGENDARY GENERALS

Seventy-five years before I was born, a gallant Army general appeared in the land of America in 1885. His name was George Patton, a Lieutenant General in the US Army. I share some spectacular similarities with this gallant man. First of all, both of us were born in the eleventh month of the year, which is November. Another thing is that both of us have fathers who were veterans who knew and experienced real battle.

Thirdly, both of us like sports very well. I have won numerous medals in track events as a student at the university and as a young officer. I still run up to ten kilometres every week. I became interested in sports right from Form One in Teachers' College Potiskum. I

With my South African counterpart Lt General Lindile Yam hunting game in South Africa. In front of us is a blue wildebeest I killed with a single shot. Hunting has always been my hobby.

won several awards in sports. I still treasure the Silver Medal I won in the 1990 NUGA sports competition.

I am the kind of person who doesn't joke with my physical fitness and I consider it mandatory to compliment mental fitness with physical fitness. Mental fitness alone is not good enough. Physical fitness alone is also not good enough. One must be physically and mentally fit. One thing that I reinvigorated in the Army is drills and regular exercise to keep my officers and soldiers fit and alert. I find it ridiculous and repulsive to see an officer or a soldier with a pot belly or anything that shows that he or she is not physically fit. It is for this reason that I made it a habit to always admonish officers and soldiers to take drills and regular exercise as a lifetime habit. And I don't just say it, I show it to them through my life.

As officer cadet with MM Adamu

One of the things I have learned from General Patton is always to do everything you ask of those you command. This has always been my cardinal principle in command and all leadership responsibilities. I lead by example. Talk is cheap, and in most cases ineffective. When I talk to soldiers and officers about physical exercise, I always sum it up with a practical example.

Now, let me tell you something very important and unique to all combat operations. This is somehow sacred, but I know some people may dispute it or label me as a religious bigot. I think all battles have an unknown factor that eventually decides who wins or loses the battle. So even though the numerical strength of the troops matters and the training and the kind of equipment are also important, appeal to some powers beyond our human scope is important. I am not the only general who holds this belief. As I told you earlier, I share a lot of things in common with General Patton.

He also had this belief about an unknown factor, usually something beyond our understanding that determines who wins or loses a battle. General Patton was a very blunt general who never minced his words. He was the kind of guy who liked to tell things the way they were.

Before he died he said: "There are three ways that men get what they want: by planning, by working, and by praying. Any great military operation takes careful planning, or thinking. Then, you must have well-trained troops to carry it out: that's working. But between the planning and the operation there is always

This picture is generally called the prophetic picture because it captured the images of three officers who became Army chiefs. In the middle is Lt. General Azubike Iherika who was at the time COAS. By his right is then Major General Kenneth Minimah who took over from General Iherika. Both Generals Ihejirika and Minimah were appointed by President Goodluck Jonathan. Behind them with a touch of red on his beret is me (General Buratai) who took over from General Minimah after I was appointed COAS by President Muhammadu Buhari in July 2015.

an unknown. That unknown spells defeat or victory, success or failure. It is the reaction of the actors to the ordeal when it actually comes. Some people call that getting the breaks; I call it God. God has His part, or margin in everything, that's where prayer comes in."

I concur with the man and I think he is just speaking my mind. I totally agree that God has his margin in everything that we humans do. After all, he owns and controls the world. I hear some folks say there is no God and I laugh when I hear such nonsense. I have never seen God, but anyone who has fought in battles knows that God exists, for there are times one gets saved from a bullet or mortar fire by the hand of providence and omnipotence. Such miraculous escapes have no logical explanation but God.

The issue of training and re-training is very important. After that, comes the vital issue of equipment and intelligence. These two go hand in hand. If you don't have the right intelligence you'll make use of your equipment in the wrong place, which in most cases is counterproductive. War is not a simple business, nor is it child's play, because of its association with death. In fact, what makes war a victory is making the enemy die for his cause or his flag. If you can confront your enemy and after some exchange of gunfire make him or her perish for his flag or ideology, then you can be judged victorious. So the loss of blood, of human life, determines who wins or loses a battle.

Most people are afraid of death, and that's okay, but it is wrong for the soldier to be afraid of death because if he fears death, it will consume him like a shark. For

Troops of Operation Lafiya Dole diligently disarming and
removing mines planted by the insurgents

each of us, there will always come the moment when
death, like a nurse, takes us by the hand and quietly
says, "It is time to go home. Night-time is coming.
It's your bedtime, child of the earth." Until that time
comes, we have no reason to worry about death. And a
profession like the Army has no place for the cowards
who die ten thousand times before their death. Indeed,
fear has torments.

According to General Patton, and I agree with him, "No poor bastard ever won a war by dying for his country. He won it by making other bastards die for their country." Somewhat crude, but true. The death of a soldier is not something glorious because it signifies victory for the enemy. Dying for your country might be good, but living for your country is better. But as General Patton rightly said, "a real man will never let his fear of death overpower his honour, his sense of duty to his country, and his innate manhood. Battle is the most magnificent competition in which a human being can indulge. It brings out all that is best and it removes all that is base."

This then, my friend, is the secret of legendary generals. The secret is to refuse to listen to whatever is whispering to your head to make you succumb to the

Receiving the Nigerian Army flag from my predecessor Lt Gen KTJ Minimah (right) during the taking over and handing over ceremony at the Nigerian Army Headquarters on July 15 2015

fear of death and allow your honour, sense of duty and innate manhood to be trampled upon. Once you make up your mind to protect and defend your honour and that of your country no matter what, death will stay away from you, for in truth death is also a coward. It is also afraid of the brave and the courageous.

"When a resolute young fellow steps up to the great bully and takes him boldly by the beard, he is often surprised to find it comes off in his hand, and that it was only tied on to scare away the timid adventurers," said Ralph Waldo Emerson. Most of our fears are illusions. *That is why people living deeply have no fear of death.* Fear is the main source of superstition, and one of the main sources of cruelty. To conquer fear is the beginning of bravery.

Every soldier must know this. For you to conquer your fear, you must be up and doing. If you are a soldier, you must learn to attack and attack and attack after simple planning. Don't wait until you have the perfect setting to execute your plan. To stay idle and remain inactive is not good, because inaction breeds doubt and fear. Action breeds confidence and courage.

Someone sent me a quote by Frank Herbert via email when I was appointed as Chief of Army Staff and it goes like this: "I must not fear. Fear is the mind-killer. Fear is the little-death that brings total obliteration. I will face my fear. I will permit it to pass over me and through me. And when it has gone past I will turn the inner eye to see its path. Where the fear has gone there will be nothing. Only I will remain." This simple quote had truly inspired me not to listen to my fears.

The Army is not a profession for the fearful and the cowardly. Most people don't know what to be afraid of. I think they should be afraid of losing their honour and pride.

Another thing I can't bear is slackness or faint commitment to duty, which is a symptom of lack of diligence. I also believe that slackness and lack of commitment are the twin extinguishers of alertness. This is because no army, regardless of the size of its troops and sophistication of equipment, can win a war without diligence and alertness. The moment a soldier or a commander begins to exhibit slackness and faint commitment, the enemy has won.

I have a theory which I developed when I was appointed as Chief of Army Staff. The theory is this: *The diligence and alertness of an Army is directly proportional to its victory in warfare.* Again, I am on the same page with General Patton who said: "The only way you get on in this profession is to have the reputation of doing what you are told as thoroughly as possible. So far, I have been able to accomplish that…" He goes on to add that: "Alertness must be bred into every soldier. I don't give care a jot for a man who's not always on his toes."

This reminds me of a story he narrated about a German soldier who slept on guard duty and as a result gave General Patton and his troop the opportunity to kill four hundred of his fellow Germans in the Second World War. So a lack of commitment to duty or slackness by one soldier can cause the death of many. Many of the deaths and casualties troops encounter could have been avoided if they were more alert.

I think some people now join the Army for economic reasons. They simply want to get a job and earn a living. The Army is not a job you do to earn a living but rather a noble profession which is meant for the brave and the courageous. This whole thing starts and ends with the soldier, and this is why diligence must be thoroughly applied in the recruitment process. The soldier is the Army, for no Army is better than its soldiers. This is why I place so much attention on soldiers. And, don't forget that the soldier is first of all a citizen and that the highest obligation or duty of a citizen to his country is that of bearing arms for his country. So the soldier deserves all the best in terms of remuneration and welfare, because his is the noblest of all the professions. But a cowardly soldier or a slack soldier is not only a disgrace to his country; he is worse than its enemy. I would rather you give me five score brave and alert soldiers than a thousand slack

With my team on top of the Gwoza mountains taking a rest after a long walk. Sitting by my right is Major General Udoh, the Chief of Training and Operations of the Nigerian Army.

and cowardly ones. The cowardly or slack soldier is just a walking corpse; he or she can't be of any use to his formation. The brave soldier has a feeling of indestructibility in him, but the coward is already paralysed and dead because of his fear.

As a military professional one has to sacrifice a lot in terms of family life, and definitely, wives and children also have to sacrifice and face a lot of challenges. I know that even when I was in Angola, I had to leave my family alone for them to be taken care of. When I went to Bakassi, I had to leave my family, because it is not everywhere you go with the family. You have to make sure that they take care of themselves and then try to be in touch with them. I thank God for my family, because they tried to stay together in peace and unity even in my absence. As you can see, even when I go to Borno, which is my state, I find it difficult to stay with my family because there is no time for it. I have to concentrate on my primary assignment. By and large, I try to balance work and family life because both are important, but the most important thing in life is that we chose this job voluntarily so we have to give it our best. It is satisfying to say that we have been rewarded accordingly through the appreciation of Nigerians, especially through the commendation of the Commander in Chief, and this has given us great joy and we really appreciate that.

∾ LESSON ∾

All legendary generals have the vision of an eagle, the heart of a lion, the cleverness of a fox and the tenacity of a goat. They devote time to perfect generalship through patience and diligence, which eventually makes them stand out in the crowd. They are men of self-confidence and perpetual optimism.

*"The moral is to the physical
as three to one."*

Napoleon Bonaparte

CHAPTER EIGHT

❖ ❖ ❖

WE ARE IN THIS TOGETHER

As I said earlier, the Nigerian Army has defeated the armed opposition group popularly known as the Boko Haram insurgents. The sad thing is that they have run to the late Al Baghdadi to form what is now known as ISWAP, although it is not under the control of the hooligan they call Imam Abubakar Shekau. ISWAP as it is today is a network of various cells with no single mission or goal. Even though these incoherent cells appear as one single entity, the fact still remains that it is very loose-knit. There is still a residue of the real Boko Haram sect started by Yusuf, then some group that is there to further the interest of some foreign powers and their ilk, and then another faction which is there to further the interests of certain prominent politicians.

The mission of the present ISWAP is no longer the implementation of the sharia but the spreading of fear and terror. Its main motivation is filthy lucre—thus the reason ISWAP kills people with careless abandon. It kills Muslim faithful in their hundreds. The terrorists sect targets the peasant, the unemployed, the farmer, the poor neighbourhood or village but not the rich and their settlements. This is a clear diversion from the original mission of the *Jama'atul ahl lil Sunna lil Da'awati wal Jihad,* for when Yusuf started the sect he relied heavily on the peasants, the dejected, the traders and the poor neighbourhood. In fact, he stayed and operated in a poor neighbourhood and not in the Government Reserved Area (G.R.A). The poor were not his enemies, and it was not his mission to plunder and sack their villages or destroy their livelihoods. The Boko Haram of today considers the poor as persona non grata and enemy number one.

Indeed, Professor Paul Collier of Oxford University was right when he said:

> *Future civil wars will take the form of a government pitted against a private extra-legal military grouping. They will variously be called rebels, terrorists, freedom fighters, or gangsters, but their essential characteristics will be the same. These wars will also be a throwback, but to a very different period: the time before nation states cohered.*

I am an infantry general who happens to be the Chief of Staff of the Nigerian Army. The infantryman is the soldier of soldiers, for we are the ones who go on into high-stress and dangerous environment to close in with the enemy and destroy him. We were trained to march into danger if necessary. It is not an exaggeration to say that the infantry bears the heat of all battles. That does not mean other corps of the army are irrelevant, no! Every unit counts; the artillery, the armour, intelligence, engineers, all are important. When I came on board as COAS, the President, who happens to be my Commander in Chief, gave me my orders: relocate to Borno, crush the Boko Haram terrorists and restore civil authority to the area. He gave me a timeline to finish with the terrorists. I wasted no time in complying with the Presidential orders.

I quickly relocated to Maiduguri and took charge of the operations at the Theatre Command. I deprived myself of all luxuries and concentrated on one thing — defeating Boko Haram terrorists. I went to the North-East to rally the soldiers and motivate them to fight like never before. It paid off. There was a time when my convoy was ambushed by Boko Haram insurgents. Instead of withdrawing back to Maiduguri, I said, "No! We are in this together, I can't go back. We must all go together to clear the ambush." So I advanced with them, and that was how we cleared the ambush. If the Chief of Army Staff (COAS) does not turn back, who would turn and run from such an ambush?

Unfortunately, we lost one soldier, and one other soldier, a brigadier-general, was wounded in the attack.

My greatest fulfilment is with the progress that has been made in the war against Boko Haram since I was appointed. We came at a time when truly the challenge of the insurgency was very high. It was at its peak. There is no gainsaying the fact that some progress had been made before we came in, but that progress was being overtaken by the virtual resurgence of Boko Haram. At the time, there were only four local administrations that were not under the Boko Haram terrorist group's control out of about twenty-seven in Borno. It was the same in Yobe State; two local administrations were still under Boko Haram's influence. That was the situation we met when we came in July 2015.

As at today, those two local governments in Yobe state have been reclaimed from Boko Haram. And in Borno, all the LGAs that were under the influence and control of Boko Haram have been liberated and have been effectively put under the control of the elected government. The areas that are remaining are just the peripheral, which lies along the border between Nigeria and Cameroon. Especially Chad and Niger borders. No single local government is under the control of Boko Haram. To me, this is a major achievement and source of fulfilment.

∾ LESSON ∾

People like Generals Chris Abutu Garuba, Abu Ahmadu, I.D. Penap and a few others taught me that a leader must not only be good at his craft but also lead in the fore-front in times of danger. When morale is low and your people appear to be discouraged, you must be able to re-invigorate them through your style.

"War must be, while we defend our lives against a destroyer who would devour all; but I do not love the bright sword for its sharpness, nor the arrow for its swiftness, nor the warrior for his glory. I love only that which they defend."

J. R. R. Tolkien

CHAPTER nine

❖ ❖ ❖

KILLED IN ACTION, or WOUNDED IN ACTION?

I have listened with keen interest to some people who say that soldiers are still dying in this fight against insurgents even though they failed to take into cognizance the fact that for every soldier that died, at least ten insurgents also died. It is a fact that the insurgents have been killed in their thousands, but this is under reported. The propaganda machine doesn't want to report the deaths of the insurgents, for reasons that I still can't fathom.

Let me provide a simple definition of Killed-In-Action (KIA) and Wounded in Action (WIA). First of all, KIA refers to service personnel killed in the course of duty or action or died as a result of injuries sustained from that duty or action. On the other hand, WIA refers to service personnel who sustains injury in the course of his duty or action. My soldiers are fighting the

insurgents like never before; like warriors. They are doing everything to defend civilians and also confront the enemy on their behalf. It is a fact that the number of civilian casualties and non-combatants had drastically reduced. Even though we recorded some casualties in our operations, it is a fact that the death ratio of troops to the insurgents is roughly 2 to 8. In other words, for every 2 soldiers that paid the supreme price, eight insurgents also got neutralized.

In the past administration, more civilians were killed than soldiers, but now Army officers have decided to fully get involved in the fight and this is costing some of them their lives. Yet some short-sighted Nigerians who failed to have a clear view of the whole enchilada are not happy that innocent civilians are not being killed in this fight. They are not satisfied that Army officers have decided to take a stand against insurgents to the extent of dying in combat. Every soldier knows very well that there is always a possibility of being killed on the battlefront. The important thing is not to allow oneself to get killed in combat. Soldiers who are killed by explosions of improvised explosive devices (IEDs) and related incidents are not classified as KIA. It is also important that I make it clear that soldiers who were injured in battle but succeeded in reaching a medical facility are also not classed as KIA but Wounded in Action (WIA), even if they eventually die at the facility.

It is unfortunate that the Nigerian Army is dealing with an enemy who doesn't follow any conventional rules of engagement and therefore uses IEDs, kidnapping and beheading as warfare strategies. The Nigerian Army does not sanction such barbaric acts, simply because we are a conventional army. It is true that some soldiers and officers have paid the supreme price with their lives to safeguard and protect Nigeria. I consider their sacrifices sacred and their deaths tragic.

I will digress here by telling you an old story. This happened during the American Civil War that took place under the administration of President Abraham Lincoln. The President heard that a Mrs. Bixby lost five soldier sons in the war to preserve the unity of the United States. He was moved to compassion because the little grace or virtue of empathy inside him could not fathom the kind of pain this woman was passing through. Thus, he wrote the following letter to her:

"Dear Madam, I have been shown in the files of the War Department a statement of the Adjutant-General of Massachusetts, which showed that you are the mother of five sons who have died gloriously on the field of battle. I feel how weak and fruitless must be any words of mine which should attempt to beguile you from the grief of a loss so overwhelming. But I cannot refrain from tendering to you the consolation that may be found in the thanks of the Republic they died to save. I pray that our Heavenly Father may assuage the anguish of your bereavement, and leave you only the cherished memory of the loved and lost, and the solemn pride that must

be yours, to have laid so costly a sacrifice upon
the altar of Freedom. Yours, very sincerely and
respectfully, Abraham Lincoln."

You see how they do it over there? He tactfully
reminded her that these five sons had died gloriously in
battle and not the other way around, even though there
was little evidence to suggest that he was aware of the
reason and causes of their deaths in that battle. Here in
Nigeria, we take such solemn matters like the deaths
of our soldiers in war seriously and do not and play
politics with it just to score cheap propaganda points.
We don't care how this malicious journalism will affect
the families of the bereaved if they hear that their loved
ones died because of some government incompetence
or failure to supply the required equipment. Let's not
forget that propaganda and publicity are like oxygen to
the insurgents.

We sit in our homes, sipping coffee and watching
television while some soldier is out there at the
battlefront trying to kill our enemies and preserve his
life. We don't even know that if he kills our enemies,
the terrorists, and survives, this soldier will never be
the same again. To kill is not a simple business. But
don't just take that assertion from me. Let me read you
part of an account by a British private, when he had
just shot his first enemy fighter in Afghanistan in 2006.

He wrote this:

"Afterwards, I sat there and I thought 'Hang
on. I just shot someone'. I had a brew and

that. I didn't get to sleep that night. I just lay there all night thinking, 'I shot someone'. It's something strange. A really strange feeling. You feel like, you know, a bit happy with yourself—I've done my job, it's what I've come here for, know what I mean? He's Taliban and I've got one of them. You feel quite chuffed about it.

"Then you're feeling, like, you know, well you know, sad. You're thinking ... well, you know, the geezer's another human being at the end of the day. Then you get the feeling, well, you know, it's either him or me. I think people get, you know, religious then as well. You're thinking, well, in the bigger picture, if there is like a geezer up there and a geezer downstairs, what does that mean to me now that I've just shot someone? Am I going to hell or what? And all of that went through my mind that night, for hour after hour after hour."

This is what the average soldier is passing through on our behalf. The least we could do for these soldiers is to give them our unflinching support and loyalty.

✌ LESSON ✌

Insurgency and terrorism thrive on propaganda and publicity, especially of the death of government forces. The soldier's business is either to kill the enemy or die protecting Nigeria. Therefore, his life is sacred and should not be an issue to be politicized, because it can rob the country of its dignity.

"There are certain things in war of which the commander alone comprehends the importance. Nothing but his superior firmness and ability can subdue and surmount all difficulties."

Napoleon Bonaparte

CHAPTER Ten

❖ ❖ ❖

DILIGence: A sure paTH TO LeGenDary staTus

Everywhere I go I hear young people talking about success and stardom. The average Nigerian youth wants to be a success, or in most instances a celebrity. Now, because we live in perilous times, some youths have been beguiled to believe that some shaman somewhere or a religious pontiff can give them a formula or charm for success. Like most things in life, the secret to success is not something hidden or costly to obtain. The secret to success is available for anybody who means business. To succeed as an Army officer, a technocrat, a lawyer or even as a musician or an athlete, requires one critical factor. This factor is the most critical aspect of all successful achievements. No one has succeeded in any endeavour in this world without it. This factor is known as diligence. Without it, nothing can succeed; nothing will ever attract the attention of great men or make you stand before them.

The first time I came across this diligence principle was when I asked my father about the secret to success as an officer. That was in 1989, if my memory does not fail me. My father closed his eyes and remained silent for some minutes, then opened his eyes and said, "Try to be diligent my son. Diligence is everything; and everything you can do to succeed will amount to nothing without diligence."

"What is diligence, father?"

"Diligence is the earnest, conscientious application of your energy to accomplish what has been undertaken. In other words, it is the exercise of investing all your energy to completing assigned tasks. It is characterised by steady, earnest, and energetic applications and efforts. In simple terms, it means that a diligent person continually works hard towards his or her goals and makes use of what resources and opportunities are available. He or she is vigilant to avoid errors and to stay focused on the task at hand. He or she pays careful attention to details and is dedicated to achieving quality results. Diligence provides a basis for people trusting the person with jobs that are tricky or complicated. It is important to understand that diligence does not rely on talent, but employs commitment, industry, and perseverance to transform vision into reality."

"Is that so?" I said.

"Of course, my son. The concept of diligence is engraved in certain basic principles. Diligence invests time, thought, and energy into a task with the hope that it will produce a healthy return. By investing a lot, diligent individuals expect to gain a lot. They realise that what they get out of something depends upon what they are willing to put into it. Diligence does not allow a task once undertaken to remain incomplete; it rather aims at finishing the task fully. It counts the cost and sees things through to the bitter end. In fact, for the diligent person, the satisfaction of finishing a task is often as meaningful as any praise or recognition they receive from others. Diligence also applies to both small and large tasks, significant or menial, easy or difficult. It applies the same efforts to whatever task is at hand, realising that anything worth doing is worth doing right," said my father.

I asked, "How can one be diligent father?"

"A diligent person must work hard and complete all his or her assigned tasks before going to rest or relax," said the Second World War veteran.

I once asked an old Bangladeshi veteran what his advice to young people would be, both in the military and civilian circle, for the achievement of personal success. He replied, "As for any specific advice, I know a very old, time-tested recipe for success. Our ancestors came up with it hundreds of years ago: diligence, the mother of success. I am sure that remains relevant today."

I asked him, "How can one show diligence and perseverance?"

He said, "My answer is that one should try hard no matter what the result is, because the greatest glory is not in never falling but in rising every time one falls. A champion is the one who gets up, even when he finds it tough to do so. Satisfaction lies in the effort, not in the attainment; full effort is full victory. Diligence demands three basic traits: patience, flexibility and gentleness. Tasks often involve time delays beyond one's control. Diligence accepts these challenges patiently without unnecessary worry and frustration."

Now I know better. Diligence is very important for anyone who wants to succeed as an officer. A diligent person is characterised by the determination to finish the task, do it right, follow instructions, concentrate on the work and not be lazy.

For some of you who are students in high schools and tertiary institutions, I think the admonition of Abigail Adams, wife of John Adams, 2nd President of the United States (1735-1826), will make more sense to you. She said, "Learning is not attained by chance, it must be sought for with adoration and attended to with diligence."

I totally agree with Samuel Johnson, the English poet (1709-1784), who said: "Few things are impossible to diligence and skill." This is what most of us fail to understand, and this is what is hindering us from success. Just take a look at the life and time of the late Michael Jackson, Hakeem Olajuwon, the basketball player, Steve Jobs, the father of Apple, President Muhammadu Buhari and General Colin Powell of the United States and you will realise that all they did was to combine diligence and skill. If you do the same thing, you will join their league. If you don't, you will never be like them.

What makes me stand out from the crowd is not just my height or brains and character but diligence and courage in the discharge of my duties and responsibilities. Despite the fact that my birth was foretold some four hundred years before I was born, God's mercy has been with me since childhood. Diligence and courage helped and guided me to reach my present status.

∾ LESSON ∾

Diligence is at the root of every success. Without it, no one can succeed in any worthwhile endeavour. It is good to have talent or a good family with all the right social connections, but if you refuse to be diligent in your pursuits, you will end up as a failure. And don't confuse diligence with persistence, because the two are not the same. Diligence, to my mind, is the combination of persistence, skill, wisdom and patience.

"The commander must establish personal and comradely contact with his men, but without giving away one inch of authority."

General Erwin Rommel

CHAPTER ELEVEN

❖ ❖ ❖

Super Camp and Offensive Operations

"In war, the only sure defence is offensive, and the efficiency of the offence depends on the warlike souls of those conducting it."

General George S. Patton Jr. in 'War as I Knew It'

One thing that has become a major decisive factor in the defeat of the Boko Haram insurgency is what I called the Super Camp strategy, which the Nigerian Army conceptualized and implemented in 2019. Super Camp is all about creating a means or platform to serve as a launching pad for mobile offensive operations in containing and denying the Boko Haram insurgents' freedom of action in identified areas across the theatre. It is an audacious plan because it is simple, but it needs to be boldly executed.

Gallant troops of Operation Lafiya Dole in clearance
and rescue operations in Borno, 2019.

One of the characteristics of a good commander or general is the ability to develop bold, inventive plans that produce decisive results. Commanders demonstrate audacity by violently applying combat power. They understand when and where to take risks and do not hesitate as they execute their plan. Commanders dispel uncertainty through action; they compensate for lack of information by seizing the initiative and pressing the fight. Audacity inspires soldiers to overcome adversity and danger (Fisher, 2014).

Super Camp is necessary in combating insurgents because of its unique ability to provide the Army with an effective channel for decisive operations. When I say decisive offensive operations, I mean attacks that conclusively determine the outcomes of major operations, battles, and engagements. At the operational level, decisive operations achieve the goals of each phase of a campaign. Ground operations within campaigns may include several phases. Within each phase is a decisive operation. Its results substantially affect the course of the campaign. At the tactical level, decisive battles or engagements achieve the purpose of the higher headquarters mission. Commanders win decisive operations through close combat that physically destroys the enemy, overcomes his will to resist, or seizes, occupies, and retains terrain (Fisher, 2014).

Super Camps would further boost force protection of troops while on camps, as well as enable them to project force through long distance patrols and ambushes to dominate their areas of operation. It is important and timely because the Army needs to be on the offensive if we are to silence the insurgents and overwhelm them. This is because the offence is the decisive form of war because of its unique ability to destroy the enemy especially the remnants of the insurgents that are lurking around in some parts of northern Borno.

Super Camp usually goes hand in hand with a tactical road march. In fact, Super Camp is always a result of a tactical road march, because when we have a rapid relocation of troops from disadvantageous locations to an area of strength so that they can concentrate and conserve resources and power to effectively deal with the enemy, it is then that we can say we have a Super Camp. A 'tactical road march' is a rapid movement used to relocate units within an area of operations to prepare for combat operations. Tactical road marches occur when a force must maintain security or when movements occur within range of enemy influence. Commanders may still execute tactical road marches in low-threat situations.

Gallant Nigerian troops on the move for final clearance operation in Sambisa, 2019.

Super Camp came about because, apart from intelligence gathering, it is the only sure path to seizing, retaining and exploiting the initiative to decisively defeat the insurgents. Although many people didn't understand the concept and its modus operandi, the results that it is yielding in the theatre are enough to convince everyone that it is a step in the right direction. It has completely shifted the dynamics of the fight against insurgency by its unique ability to confound the insurgents. They no longer have the initiative and the availability of soft targets or weak links in our formations for them to exploit is no longer there. Our troops are concentrated in the Super Camps, and they are impenetrable to the insurgents. But what is giving the insurgents sleepless nights is that the troops are not just concentrated in the Super Camps but continuous, offensive attacks like raids and ambush are carried out against the insurgents non-stop. What I really wanted is for our troops to launch a simultaneous attack on the insurgents in such a manner that they would be thrown off balance. This is exactly what has been happening. The insurgents are overwhelmed because all their major defences have been disrupted. This is why many of them are being eliminated, while some are surrendering to us. In a nutshell, the Super Camp strategy of offensive attack through the concentration of forces was conceived to achieve the following results:

- Disrupting enemy coherence
- Securing or seizing terrain
- Denying the enemy resources
- Fixing the enemy
- Gaining information
- Protecting the people

The troops of the Nigerian Army had no doubt routed and defeated the insurgents, but like a vicious snake passing through its death throes, the insurgents are still conducting hit and run attacks. This is why the Army can no longer afford to be on the defensive and wait

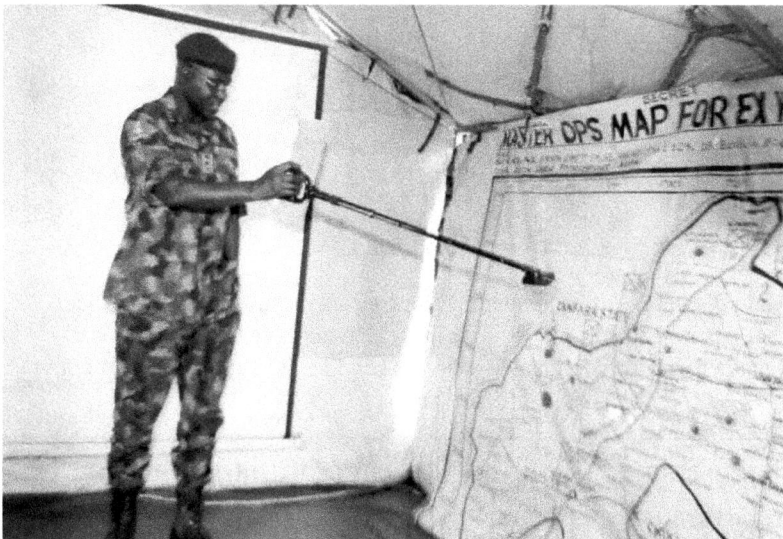

Explaining a point to some officers in Kaduna in 2017

With General AA Tarfa then Commander, Armour Corps

Major General Udoh expounding the concept of Super Camp to officers of Operation Lafiya Dole in Damboa, Borno State. General Udoh is another warrior-commander who has been in and out of the theatre of operations.

for the enemy. We must seize the initiative and be on the offensive. The most important thing to do at this stage is attack and attack and attack the enemy and his formations. According to Fisher (2014), an attack is an offensive operation that destroys or defeats enemy forces, seizes and secures terrain, or both. The Super Camp offensive attacks operation was planned to help the Army achieve the following objectives:

- Spoil the plan of the enemy
- Counter-attack the enemy
- Raid the hideouts of the enemy
- Ambush the enemy in places they never anticipated
- Deceive the enemy, and lastly
- Demonstrate strength and power over the enemy.

Prior to the launch of Super Camp, our troops were scattered all over the northern parts of Borno, precisely along the fringes of the Nigeria-Niger, Nigeria-Chad and Nigeria-Cameroon borders, and because the insurgents have international collaborators and safe havens in some of these countries, they find it easy to identify weak formations, after which they mobilize their forces to attack such weak formations and units. What we did through Super Camp is the elimination of all formations and units that are weak so that they will no longer be targets for attack and exploitation for the insurgents. Instead of staying put in some of these areas, exposing themselves to enemy attacks, they now launch raids and offensive attacks on the insurgents. The insurgents and their informants no longer have the upper hand because they don't know what step the Army is going to take, where it will launch an ambush

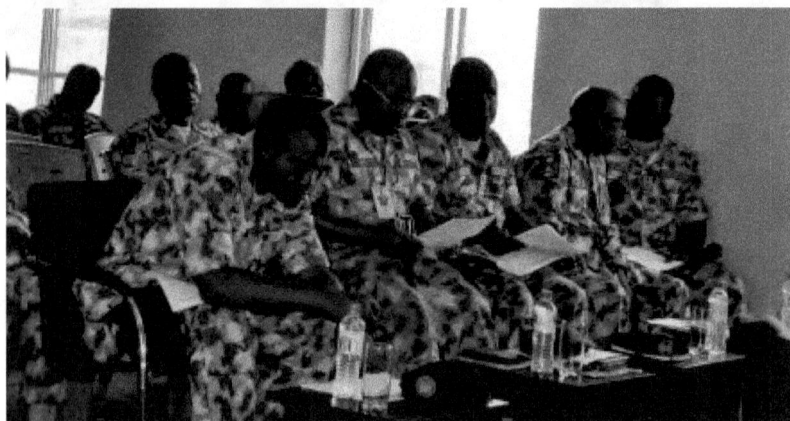

A cross section of officers listening attentively as Major General Udoh
expounding the Super Camp strategy

and so on. But some ill-informed people who don't
really know the technicalities involved in asymmetrical
warfare like the one we are fighting in northern Borno
went to town saying that the Army had withdrawn
its forces from the areas it once protected so that the
insurgents can have freedom to operate. This is a total
fallacy. What we have done is to create Super Camps

and from them launch a series of offensive attacks, raids and ambushes on the insurgents.

Gambari (2019) believes that guns and bullets alone cannot totally defeat insurgency, except in Angola, where the elimination of Jonas Savimbi led to the collapse of the UNITA armed opposition group. This is in tandem with Thompson (1966) who argued that any government that wants to defeat insurgency must do the following:

- Have a clear political aim, which in this case is that the government must show interest in negotiating with the leaders of the insurgency with a view to finding a long-lasting political solution to the insurgency. Gambari (2019) observed that if at the end of all military struggles, warring factions eventually come to the negotiation table to find common ground that can enable them to develop short and long term political solutions to their problems, why wait for so long?

- The government must function in accordance with the law. The government already has legitimacy because it is democratically elected by the majority of Nigerians in an election which the civil societies and the international community adjudged to be free and fair. The government is working according to the rule of law and our operations in the theatre of operations are also in tandem with the rules of engagement of military operations.

- The government must have an overall plan. The administration of President Buhari had come up with the Buhari Plan since 2016, when it launched the defunct Presidential Committee on the North-East Initiative, which has now been transformed into the North-East Development Commission. It is an all-encompassing plan formulated to address the root causes and after-effects of the insurgency through short and long-term strategies. The Nigerian Army University, Biu, is also part of the Buhari Plan for the North-East because it will strategically address the issue of education, manpower development and contextualized solutions to the problem.

■ The government must give priority to defeating political subversion, not the insurgents. In other words, defeating the people who serve as soldiers of the insurgency should not be the primary priority of the government but defeating the whole system and the shadowy characters behind it.

■ The government must secure its base areas first. This we have done though collaboration with other government security agencies and also through the Super Camp.

Since I am not a politician but a soldier whose primary duty is to safeguard the territorial integrity of Nigeria from all kinds of external aggression, low-intensity conflicts, insurgency and the rest, I will not waste time thinking about political solutions to this crisis but use military might to defeat them until they are totally incapacitated. We have already achieved that in places like Adamawa, Yobe, Gombe, Bauchi and a substantial part of Borno. We shall do the remaining part of Borno.

Those remnants of the insurgents that are lurking around in fringes of the border between Borno and Chad/Cameroon/Niger republics are presently receiving hard knocks through the Super Camp. I believe that isolating insurgents and terrorists from their bases of support (some towns and villages in northern Borno) is probably the most important element of successful campaigns against them.

We are carrying out aggressive patrolling, ambushes, raids and continuous offensive bombardments on the insurgents wherever they are. We don't need to be one hundred percent sure of our intelligence to carry out these operations. Once we are sure that we have between sixty to seventy percent accuracy of our intelligence, we move in to attack the insurgents. This has helped us to limit the mobility and range of the insurgents, which in effect means that we have taken away their space and their time. Many of the insurgents are now coming out to surrender themselves to the Army, while the few that are holding out are dying of starvation and misery in the bush.

When we started the Super Camp, some unscrupulous elements in the local media, and especially the international media, gave it a bad name. They said that the Army had withdrawn from all its formations in the theatre of operations, leaving locales at the mercy of the marauding insurgents. I will say this is mischievous. Publicity is like oxygen to the insurgents. Once we can remove this "oxygen of publicity," we can increase other aspects of counterinsurgency and the gaining of popular support. Now that everyone is witnessing

A cross section of officers deliberating on the Super Camp
strategy in Damboa.

the potency and efficacy of the Super Camp, many of
the local media, but mostly the international media,
suddenly decided to keep mute.

What is important for people to know is that our
commanders carry out massive offensive onslaughts
on the marauding insurgents based on tactical actions
and credible intelligence. These tactical commanders
concentrate on designing offensive land operations
after determining what objectives will achieve decisive
results, where troops will operate, the relationships
among subordinate forces in time and purpose, and
where to apply the decisive effort.

The purpose of these tactical operations which we
have launched through Super Camp is to attack the
insurgents' centre of gravity through simultaneously

or sequentially attacking their decisive points. Mass effects of joint and multinational forces allow us to seize the initiative because it denies the insurgents freedom of action, disrupts their sources of strength, and creates the conditions for operational and tactical success.

CHARACTERISTICS OF OFFENSIVE OPERATIONS CARRIED OUT BY SUPER CAMPS

1. The offensive attacks are characterised by surprise, concentration, tempo, and audacity. Our commanders and troops attack the insurgents at a place or time they never expect or in a situation they are unprepared to face or cope with. As General Patton said in *War As I Knew It*, estimating the enemy commander's intent and denying him the ability to gain thorough and timely situational understanding is necessary to achieve surprise. Unpredictability and boldness help gain surprise. By diminishing enemy combat power, surprise enables attackers to exploit paralysis and hesitancy. The man is right because sudden, violent and unanticipated attacks have a paralyzing effect on the insurgents.

2. We usually ensure that these offensive operations are carried out based on accurate intelligence and other relevant information regarding the insurgents, weather, and terrain. Commanders manoeuvre their forces to advantageous positions before contact.

3. We try to see that the insurgents don't have access to accurate information about our operations through the use of highly effective defensive information operations (IO). We only allow them to see what we want them to see or hear. In this way, we can keep or inhibit the enemy from acquiring accurate information about friendly forces.

4. Contact with enemy forces before the decisive operation is deliberate, designed to shape the optimum situation for the decisive operation.

5. The decisive operation is a sudden, shattering action that capitalizes on subordinate initiative and a common operational picture (COP) to expand throughout the AO. Commanders execute it violently without hesitation to break the enemy's will or destroy him.

For those who have been carefully following developments in the theatre of operations in the north-east, they will realise that one of the strategies that I have been using is the control of tempo of war to confuse and confound the enemy so that I can always have the initiative and the upper hand. For example, the Theatre Commanders (TCs) that I usually post to the theatre consist of officers of different tempos. This is because controlling or altering tempo is necessary to retain the initiative in every war especially insurgencies.

These pictures show Lt General Buratai with troops during operations against Boko Haram terrorists at the Nigerian Army Special Super Camp Ngamdu, Borno State, in April 2020.

✁ LESSON ✁

One must be innovative in tactics and operations to neutralize insurgents because of the asymmetric nature of their attacks. Innovation is crucial in modern day warfare.

"Animals are such agreeable friends — they ask no questions; they pass no criticisms."

George Eliot

CHAPTER TWELVE

❖ ❖ ❖

MY Encounters
WITH snakes

I hear a lot of people talk about my relationship with snakes. Some say I am a snake charmer. Others say I own a snake farm. A few others say I keep snakes for ritual purposes. Well, the truth of the matter is that yes, I own a snake farm. That's correct, but I am not a snake charmer and neither do I use snakes for rituals. I should like to say there is nothing evil about snakes and I consider them as bona fide members of the animal kingdom created by God.

I have had strange encounters with snakes all my life. They started when I was just a little boy of thirteen years old, and we went to hunt for birds in the bushes. I remember that it was in 1973. I tried to scare it to run, but when it got defensive, I backed off. I had another encounter with a snake in Angola in 1994, on the last day I was to leave and come back to Nigeria. I almost stepped on the snake while jogging along the road and had to jump over it. I also had another mysterious encounter with a snake again in 1996; this time I found one inside my staff car. I was a Major then. How did it get inside the car? Was it a spirit that transformed itself into a snake? Maybe it saw a small opening and managed to crawl into the car. My weirdest encounter with a snake was in 2006 when I saw a snake inside my bathroom.

Of all my encounters with snakes, it was one I had in 1994 that changed my perception about them.

An incident involving great bravery and courage happened around that time. It involved two American Delta Force soldiers. A Black Hawk helicopter had crashed inside enemy territory on October 3, 1993, in Mogadishu. The crew were in great danger and if help didn't reach them as quickly as possible, all of them would perish in the hands of the enemy. The soldiers, Master Sergeant Gary I. Gordon and Sergeant First Class Randall D. Shughart, did the unthinkable. They requested to be inserted at the crash site of the down Black Hawk helicopter to protect the lives of the helicopter crew. Their request was denied twice but they were able to have their way after much persistence. They got inserted into the fighting zone and proceeded to protect the sole survivor, pilot Chief Warrant Officer, Michael Durrant. Gordon and Shughart defended Durant from the attacks of the Somalis. They were eventually killed, but Durrant was taken captive.

For their actions, Gordon and Shughart were presented with the Medal of Honour posthumously (Congressional Medal of Honour Society, 1994a,

1994b).Their story motivated me as a young army officer to be brave and courageous and if possible to risk my life to save my comrades. In that same 1993, I went to Zimbabwe on a holiday in (1993) and decided to visit one of the tourist attractions, the very popular Harare Snake Park. I saw the way they kept snakes and how interested people were in coming to see them. It was very interesting and they had different species of snakes. It was there that I got the idea of starting a snake farm in Nigeria.

Snakes are legless carnivorous reptiles which are covered with overlapping scales. To accommodate their narrow bodies, snakes' paired organs (such as kidneys) are placed one in front of the other instead of side by side, and most have only one functional lung. Some species retain a pelvic girdle with a pair of vestigial claws on either side of the cloaca. I have a statue of an Egyptian cobra.

Now, let me tell you a few things you need to know about snakes. First of all, they are more afraid of you than you are of them. They see humans as a potential threat. No snake wants a confrontation with human beings, because humans are bigger. They will defend themselves if they feel threatened, but if we leave them alone, they'll leave us alone. That means that if you encounter a snake in the woods, you should observe it from a distance. It's okay to appreciate wildlife in its natural surroundings, but stay at least six feet away from it—the further away you are from the snake, the more the snake will appreciate it. And if the snake seems agitated, walk away.

Secondly, snakes don't care about the kind of noise you make to frighten them because they can't hear. So making a lot of noise doesn't frighten them at all. Snakes lack external ear openings and are deaf to airborne sounds, so they won't hear or be afraid of pure noise. However, they can feel vibrations through the ground extremely well, so if you are treading heavily, snakes might feel the vibrations through the ground.

Some people say if a snake bites you, suck the venom out of the wound so that you won't be hurt. But the truth of the matter is that this is false. Suction is ineffective, because the amount of venom you remove is minute.

I am aware of the fact that no matter what I say here, some people will never like snakes. This is okay. Another man's meat is another man's poison. While many people have a fear of snakes that is irrational, many find them fascinating and keep them as pets. It's not completely absurd to fear certain snakes because snakes have always been given a bad name. There is a considerable number of people who simply don't like snakes because of one thing: venom. The fact that some snakes can kill a man with a single bite made the animal synonymous with death. This is why most people associate the reptile with death because it has killed so many people, especially in Africa and India. Snakes usually kill fifty to ninety thousand people every year.

Those who like snakes are called ophidiophiles, while having a fear of snakes is called ophidiophobia. People should fear snakes that are venomous, especially cobras and rattlesnakes, because they can potentially hurt or even kill. A lot of people have been killed because of their carelessness or recklessness with snakes. Snakes don't really want to harm human beings, but they can bite in self-defence or because they are trying to protect their space. If you come in contact with a venomous snake, or one that you think might be venomous, just leave it alone. Don't try to kill it, just walk in the opposite direction. This way, neither party gets hurt or killed.

I opened a snake farm because besides being an important part of a well-functioning ecosystem, some snakes make good pets and are good company. Saying such a thing doesn't make a person crazy. A good friend of mine once wrote, "Just as there are people who love their dogs, cats, and even rabbits and hamsters because of the company they give, that's how some people keep snakes."

Some of us who have snake farms do so because we like to have snakes around. This is because some snakes can be good companions, just like any other pets, like cats and dogs. In any case, animals like cats, dogs and snakes usually don't hurt you as human beings do. And once an animal is loyal, you can rest assured that its loyalty can never be questioned. That is one thing I like about animals. Their loyalty is never ending; it is constant. Now if it is okay to own a cat or a dog that frequently bites people, why is it that people get irritated when they see snakes as pet animals?

Another good thing about snakes is that it is cheap to keep them, because they don't eat much and don't demand specialised food like some pets. There's not much to keeping a snake once you have your basic husbandry skills down. Snakes are not fed daily—in most cases, adult snakes get fed once every seven to ten days.

There's a bit more to it than that which I must mention. While snakes are solitary animals and perfectly happy when left alone, handling them at least twice a week is important to keep them used to getting picked up by humans. It's important to have a pet snake that is docile and easy to handle and that it feeds when scheduled. A non-stressed snake feeds eagerly in captivity and doesn't give any problems in that area. On the other hand, a non-feeding snake can cause the owner some stress.

Not to worry—if the snake is healthy, isn't stressed out, and its enclosure is set up the right way, it'll eventually eat. Sometimes snakes take fasting breaks for no clear reason. At a closer look, such fasts are often associated with the biological breeding clock in their brains. They'll come out of it in a month or so, although some snakes, such as ball pythons, are known to take breaks in feeding for as long as nine months.

So, the secret to handling snakes is not to fear them at all. Be at ease and show confidence in yourself as a human being, a superior being. And don't approach them with the intent of harming them.

While some snakes don't like being handled, many captive-bred specimens tolerate it. I'm also convinced by all the years I've kept snakes as pets that some snakes don't mind being handled at all. Some even seem to enjoy it, and some are extremely friendly. While it is tempting to name a number of snakes known for their docile temperament, I'll resist the thought. The reason is that a snake's temperament can't always be judged by its species. It's more like from one individual snake to the next.

A docile snake that doesn't move makes a great alternative to a lapdog. You can even take a walk with it outside while it rests on your shoulders. Some snakes can lie on your lap happily for an extended period. There are lots of ways to spend quality time with your pet snake.

They can also help you with security. Can you imagine a burglar breaking into a dark house and turning his flashlight on only to find himself in a room filled with snakes? He may choose another house to rob and skip yours. Yes, some people are that afraid of snakes. In such cases, I don't see it as such a bad thing.

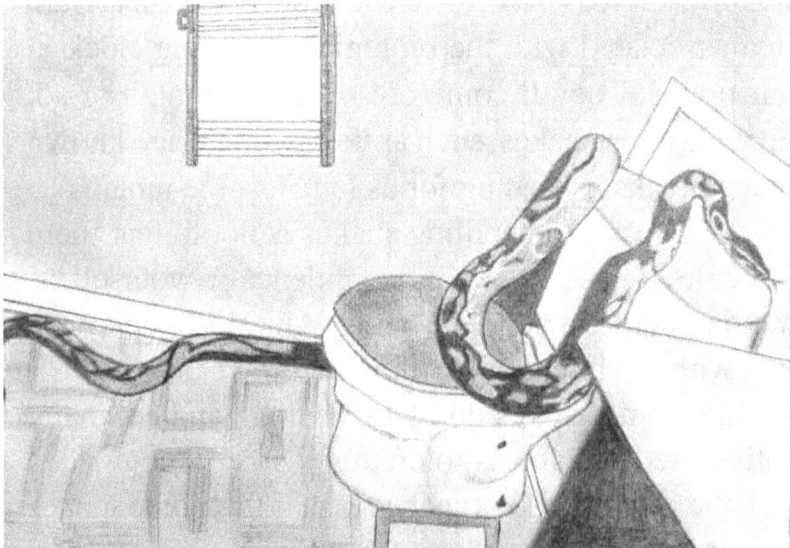

When a snake appeared in my bathroom.

∾ LESSON ∾

There is nothing special about handling snakes or keeping them. Snakes can be good pets like dogs and cats, although most people are afraid of them and don't want to have anything to do with them. The truth of the matter is that snakes are not that harmful and there is a secret to handling them. The secret is to banish fear; once you take away fear from your heart, and muster confidence, the snake will submit.

"I fully believe in ghosts. I have, my entire life. The first house I ever lived in was haunted. There was a grave of a man in the backyard. I was just a baby then, but my parents would tell me that every night, at the same time, they would hear someone walking up the stairs."

Meaghan Rath

CHAPTER THIRTEEN

❖ ❖ ❖

Encounters
WITH GHOSTS

Ghostly encounters are often associated with strange sensations, time distortions and hallucinations. I have had several encounters with ghosts — I mean different types of ghosts. Now I don't really know if it is true that a ghost is the spirit or soul of a dead person that can appear to the living. In fact, I still don't really agree that all ghosts are the spirits of dead persons trying to make contact with the living. I think a ghost could even be a jinn. In my opinion, ghosts can either be the spirits of dead people or demonic ghosts, which exist only to torment or tempt the living. What I know is that translucent entities, composed of a misty, airy or subtle material, and sometimes barely visible wispy shapes, have appeared to me from the time I was a youth. Ghosts can also be people without physical form who behave like human beings. Ghosts are sometimes called apparitions or spirits.

In many traditional accounts, ghosts were thought to be deceased people looking for vengeance (vengeful ghosts), or those who had been imprisoned on earth for bad things they did during life. The appearance of a ghost has often been regarded as an omen or portent of death. Seeing one's own ghostly double or "fetch" is a related omen of death.

I hear that some people are insinuating that ghost sightings may be related to degenerative brain diseases such as Alzheimer's disease, or such things as sleep disorders. I beg to disagree. The truth of the matter is that ghosts exist and ghost sightings are not a sign of any disease. Such paranormal activities have been happening since time immemorial. Spirits, jinns and ghosts, or whatever you want to call them, had appeared to many people in both the religious and secular world. I remember a time when it was common for people in Maiduguri to talk about an apparition known as *Mairam kuru* (White Ladies). White ladies were reported to appear in many rural areas, and were supposed to have died tragically or suffered trauma in life.

Now, let me tell you about my encounters with paranormal entities. It happened when I was a student at Government Teachers' College, Potiskum. You know at that period, we were writing exams and virtually throughout the term there was no light; even the rural electricity that was provided by the Rural Electrification Board was not available at that time. We never had an electric power supply. As a result, when we wrote our

Grade III exams, we never had the opportunity to use light to read our books at night. That was in 1978.

Okay, we were writing our Grade III exams in 1978 and everyone was serious about it. Naturally, I like to read; maybe because I am the reserved type. I find it refreshing to get myself engrossed in my books. I am not the kind of person who likes to play with words. I have come to realise that there are certain people who just like to talk about anything, even when their words don't make sense at all. I might be wrong, but I think too much noise is not good and has the potential to run a person down.

So what we normally did was to read outdoors with our lamps because of the harsh weather. One evening when we went out to read during Prep, we read outdoors until it was midnight. It was during the hot season and there was no light in the classrooms. We often carried our hurricane lanterns, tables and chairs to the field or outside the classroom for fresh air. That day I got engrossed in my studies during Prep. I was reading something on the Principles of Education and I understood what I was reading in the class. I took my table and chair to the field and continued reading after the school Prep period. Some other students joined me. Exams were approaching, and most of us wanted to score good grades.

I was so focused on my studies that by the time I raised my head, it was already twelve midnight. I had been left alone. I took a close look at my surroundings and realised that there was nobody there. All the other students had packed and gone to the hostel. I was the only one left in the dark of night. But I saw one person inside one of the classrooms with his lantern. I picked up my lantern and books, leaving the table and the chair there, and walked to the hostel. I walked confidently but very cautiously. I went to the hostel, placed my lantern by the bedside locker, lay on the bed and was waiting for sleep to come. While I was walking down to the hostel, I didn't hear the movement of anybody following me and I didn't see anything shadowy.

I was half asleep and half-awake as if my body wanted to sleep but my mind was fully awake. Then, as I was about to close my eyes and doze off, something very strange and very weird happened. In the still of the night when other students were snoring and some were whispering incoherent words, I had a paranormal encounter.

It started with a tap on my shoulder. It was an authoritative tap, as if the entity making it was tapping an errand boy. I was lying on my right side, so I had the tap on my left shoulder and arm. I have always been the kind of person who is always alert no matter what. I just woke up, and the lantern was still shining because I had not dimmed it. And then I saw a face — a horrible face covered with the aura of danger, with wild eyes and hairy. It looked at me straight in the face, into my eyes.

Instead of shivering and shouting for help, I looked straight into its eyes. I was taken aback, but I was not frightened. I was trying to find out what this being was. It stared at me again, to frighten me, and I stared back at it without any iota of fear. It blinked and stared back at me again. At that moment, the horrible ghost was intent on its resolve to terrify me. I kept staring back at it and after the third time it realised that I wasn't frightened. I think it was a clash of spirits — that of the ghost or jinn or whatever, with mine.

When the entity realised that my spirit was a strong one that was not ready to tremble and bow to it, it gave up. The entity just slumped, as if it had gone back into a vapour form, and disappeared. My bed was second from the dormitory door, so it came through the bed of the first person, and then it just retreated and left through the door.

For some time, I had me the impression that it was the occupant of the first bed who had appeared as a ghost because it bore a semblance of his face. It seemed likely that the ghost was trying to sow the seed of discord between myself and the occupant of the first bed. Another person could have concluded that the occupant of the first bed was a wizard or something of that nature, but I know the boy was innocent and clean. I was taken aback by the mysterious ways of spiritual beings, the lack of limitation they have when it comes to movement, the freedom they enjoy, their self-confidence, pride, and apparent disdain for humans.

What I then did was to wake up the boy in the first bed and ask him if he was aware of what had transpired. I said, "Come! What is happening?"

"What happened?" The boy retorted.

He didn't know what had happened. Something horrible had come to terrify me and it came through his bed, yet he didn't know what had happened? I was annoyed. I just brought down my curtain and dimmed the light of the hurricane lantern, then went off to sleep. I slept like a baby, with no fear. No fear at all - honestly. It was just natural.

I am not given to fear, especially of paranormal occurrences and encounters. In fact, paranormal encounters simply generate a lot curiosity in me to find out more information about the spiritual entities. Ghosts like jinni are a complicated subject. Some of them could be good and some could be bad. I should like to say that the one that came to scare me in the hostel was not a good one. In any case, most children of those days knew about ghosts and jinnis. You know, those folktales and so on.

I also read the stories of brave men like Iliya Dan Mai Karfi and others. *The Story of Iliya Dan Maikarfi* and his encounter with the three angels, Wargaji and Gijigiji impressed me the most. In it, I saw the fusion of wisdom, strength and compassion. All of these stories influenced me not to fear paranormal beings. I still remember I was in Form 3. Nobody knew about this story until much later when I narrated it to some friends and I think I mentioned it in one of our meetings in Abuja. So that's the black ghost that appeared to me in my hostel in 1978 at Teachers College, Potiskum. It is good to be brave and fearless, because only God knows what could have happened to me if I had been terrified and shouted from fear. That doesn't mean I am reckless. I know there is a lot of difference between recklessness and fearlessness.

Some time in 2018 a journalist asked me this question: "One thing that is synonymous with you is bravery. No one can dispute that. This bravery, is it genetic?"

"I don't know, you guys should analyse and find out. Maybe in your research, I don't know how you can confirm that bravery has anything to do with genetics," I said.

I think bravery has something to do with both nature and nurture, even though people like General Patton tend to see it as hereditary. Perhaps that was why he said he wished that cowardly soldiers should be killed in battle so that they wouldn't return to America to give birth to more cowards. According to him, the brave soldiers who survive will go back and give birth to more brave men. He might be right. But I think self-confidence, birth order, intuition, belief system, training and empathy have a lot do with bravery and courage.

Little did I know that I was not yet done with ghosts and jinni, for in 1980, when I was about to write my Grade II exams, another paranormal encounter happened. Because I was the Captain of the House (Kaigama House), I had my reserved corner. All House Captains had this as part of leadership privilege. It was in the same Teachers College, Potiskum, but this time around there was light. The school had been upgraded to a College of Education, yes, the Federal College of Education, Potiskum. So at that period, there was light. They always put on the light, even at night, even while we slept they left the lights on. They hardly took it off in the night. Both the school and the township enjoyed electricity at that time.

On this very day, I went to sleep after my studies, I laid my body on the bed and placed my head on the pillow and was about to go to sleep when I discovered that an apparition was flinging me up and down, as if I was flying. This experience has nothing to do with any type of sleeping disorder, for I was wide awake when it happened. The ghost would come and pick me up, fly with me, and drop me down.

I understand that the whole encounter was a spiritual experience and not really a bodily one. In any case, we humans are first of all spiritual entities which are clothed with this body of clay and dust. I would just be struggling with the disembodied spirit of the dead person. It's something that I can't explain properly, because I lack the proper words to express the whole experience. At times, they pressed me so hard that I would shout, and it was as though my shout wasn't audible for others to hear, although deep inside I would shout at the top of my voice. And if I managed to sleep, early in the morning before the early morning prayers, the same thing would happen. Sometimes it would be very difficult to sleep. I would say to myself *sotto voce*, "God! If I sleep, these things will come and start disturbing me again." I was the only one in my corner, but there were other students in the hostel. I was within the hostel, but in a separate corner. It went on for weeks until I managed to overcome it.

I had read *One Thousand and One Nights*, sometimes known as *Arabian Nights*, which contains a number of ghost stories often involving jinni, ghosts and corpses, so I had some knowledge about what was happening. What I didn't understand was why ghosts were attracted to me, or why they were disturbing me. I resorted to prayers and the recitation of scriptures to overcome the ghosts. That was when I knew that prayers can be very efficacious in warding off spirits. I was free for some time.

What baffles me about ghosts is the apparent ineffectiveness of physical beings to fight them because they are not physical entities but spiritual beings. That is why I had to resort to prayers. I had to continue prayers on and on. Even as it was happening, I used to pray to have relief but after sometimes, it would come back again. But the prayers helped me to have some peace and concentrate on my studies. So that was how I managed to pass my exams and leave the school.

And that was followed by my third experience, in 1980. Another bout with the white ghost started. This time around it was in the village, because as soon as I finished school, I went to my local government area council and was given an appointment as a class teacher. I was posted to Buratai to teach in the local elementary school. I had a house to myself and I think I was somewhat comfortable with the premises. I was the only person in that house, and it was somehow a very lonely compound. There was an empty room next to me, then an open space. Each time I came into the room in the evening to sleep after spending the evening with my friends, as soon as I lay down, they would come. I would hear their movements from the door. The ghosts would start to hit me, slap me and sometimes give me a serious beating. I think the ghosts simply hadn't moved on, literally or figuratively. Something from their past—often a grudge or unfinished business—holds them there. They're not going anywhere until that's resolved.

I would struggle to fight back, but to no avail. It was as if I was enjoying the conflict, and I never for a day exhibited fear to the apparitions. I think they were not happy with that; they wanted me to panic, to scream, to shout for fear, but it didn't happen. After some time, I got fed up with the whole business. Two weeks later, I complained to my older brother. I described my ordeal, and he reasoned with me and quickly got me another house.

Surprisingly, after I moved out from the hitherto haunted house, the manifestations stopped. Maybe that place was their den or enclave. For two weeks in the new house, I never complained. In the former house, I would wake up in the morning and go to my place of work. My friends would come and while away time with me in the house, but whenever I saw them off and went back to sleep, trouble would start. I wasn't scared, but I was getting tired with the way the ghosts were disturbing me.

One evening a friend visited me, and we decided to go out to have some fun and fresh air. As we went out of the gate and passed the large baobab tree, something I cannot clearly explain happened, something that made me to turn back. And as I turned back, I saw a very white thing, an apparition, a ghost. As I looked up at it, I couldn't see the top of it, it was so high. I quickly turned back and kept on moving. I didn't tell anybody what I had seen because if I had told them, they would have got scared and everyone would have run. I did not turn back, but kept on moving until we got to the road.

After our outing that night, I came back the same way and entered the house. I didn't see the apparition that had been lurking near the baobab. I went inside my room, but without the usual beating.

There was another experience with apparitions in 2001, and it happened near Owo when I was returning from Lagos. I left Lagos that day very late after observing afternoon prayers; it was a Friday. It was from the mosque that I took my vehicle and started driving down to Abuja, where my family lived. On the way, just after passing Ibadan on the road to Ile Ife, I had an accident. I had to stay there to fix the car. It was on the outskirts of Ibadan.

By the time I had finished, it was 9 pm or thereabouts. I decided to go to Ondo and get accommodation for the night. There was a road I had followed once—Owo, linking to Okene. Then I thought of a better alternative to take me to Abuja. "Kai! See the junction; why can't I follow it? It is shorter and I can find my way," I mumbled suddenly.

I passed through that road only once, but I decided to pass through it again. After about ten minutes' drive, I began to approach a hill. I saw an animal that I can't describe; the head was something else. It was a big animal. That was the only time I felt truly afraid. I was scared, and I was the only person on that road. I managed to keep my hands steady on the steering and kept on focusing on my destination. I was very alert that very night. There was no moonlight and no stars were visible. It was total darkness—but as usual, God saved me. The vicious-looking crawling ghost left me when I was about to get to my location. I took the bypass route through Obajana and arrived in Abuja at 4 am.

I have heard and read a lot of stories about paranormal beings and experiences, and I think they are real—the Anunnakis, the Alumbrados and what is popularly referred to as aliens.

Recently, I heard the story of a different kind of being in Afghanistan in 2002. The creature looked like a human being, a fully-grown man, but he was something else. It lived alone in the desert. This creature killed an entire squad of soldiers in Kandahar and this prompted the dispatch of special ops soldiers to find out what had happened to the missing squad. It was then that they found out what had happened. The soldiers walked along a ragged, mountainous trail until they arrived at the entrance to a large cave. They saw pieces of broken military equipment and gear scattered all around the clearing.

They were about to enter the cave to explore its recesses when a 13-foot, red-headed, double-toothed humanoid emerged and attacked them. According to the witnesses, the giant pierced one of the soldiers with his long spear, killing him before the rest of the squad could take him down after shooting at his face for thirty seconds straight. The body of the giant was packed and loaded into a helicopter, and transferred to a secret location in the USA for study. This creature, which is popularly known as the Giant of Kandahar, is also into cannibalism, and it is not clear if it was alone or there are other remnants of his species hovering around the world.

One particularly interesting story about a ghost that always fascinates me is that of Judith Thompson, who was very popular in Boston because of the way she killed her husband, John Alford Tyng, and a quack nicknamed Dr Blood. This happened round 1877 in Boston. Judith was a very attractive lady who worked in the home of the very wealthy Mr Tyng, and he was attracted to her. Tyng made advances towards Judith, but, being raised in a religious family, she insisted on marriage. Tyng decided he couldn't marry a servant. Besides, he was already engaged to an heiress in Boston. He came up with the idea of a secret marriage, which Dr Blood solemnized. Together they produced three children, and Mrs. Tyng grew more beautiful by the day until she became the talk of the town. Her husband was so jealous of her that he began to resent her and yearn to go and be with his Boston heiress. He did an unthinkable thing that even animals would never do; he murdered his wife and the three children and buried them. Dr Blood, who had helped him to solemnize the marriage, also helped him to kill Judith and the three children. Dr Blood was the type of person that would do anything for anyone if the price was right. It was this incident that Judith returned to as a ghost and she practically killed both Tyng and Dr Blood. True stories like these make you realise that the ghost phenomenon is a fact.

I still don't really understand why ghosts were attracted to me. Eventually, I got entangled with Mr. Xin Hui, a Chinese man who was well versed in this subject. When I asked him to explain why ghosts were attracted to me, especially in my formative years, he gave me the following answers:

"There were several. The main reasons for such an attraction are curiosity or mischief, but sometimes energy and certain astral components can also be responsible. I can only remember these offhand. Firstly, curiosity and mischief. You might just coincidentally be the one they find interesting and want to observe you as a human life. Many spirits are interested in other worlds and their social norms. They will observe you, see what you do and then when they're satisfied with their knowledge, they will leave. Mischief, however can be a bit more annoying. They'll pester you in the wee hours and disturb your sleep, pop up from time to time to give you a nice scare, or generally disturb your peace for fun and to see your reaction. They usually don't mean any harm, but they can be a pest."

Joe Nickell, a senior research fellow for the Committee for Skeptical Inquiry, which promotes scientific inquiry and critical investigation of the paranormal believes that ghosts are "all in the mind."

He said: "In the 'waking dream' state, people wake up and see a number of things—aliens, dead people, ghosts—and these are associated with feelings of dread. They'll often see the entity coming into their room, standing by their bed, or trying to choke them, and they're not able to move or talk or scream or do anything. It's a trick of the mind when the mental image is being superimposed on the actual visual scene."

I don't believe him. I think those that are sensitive to psychic gifts attract other-worldly forms to them, due to their higher vibrations and connection to the other side of the veil which separates the living and the not living.

When a ghost followed me to the hostel and tried to scare me I stared back at it, looking straight into its face. It yielded and left me alone.

∿ LESSON ∿

The human spirit is originally a valiant spirit and there is no ghost or demon that can overwhelm it if it doesn't allow fear to grip it. Therefore, we should not be afraid of paranormal experiences or entities. Mankind was never meant to be a coward.

"The Commander must be at constant pains try to keep his troops abreast of all the latest tactical experience and developments, and must insist on their practical application. He must see to it that his subordinates are trained in accordance with the latest requirements. The best form of welfare for the troops is first class training, for this saves unnecessary casualties."

General Erwin Rommel

CHAPTER FOURTEEN

❖ ❖ ❖

Be a Patriot

A lot of people don't know that I am also a poet. Yes, whenever I have time to spare or whenever the inspiration comes, I write poems to reflect or address a problem. Here is one such poem that I cherish so much and would like to reproduce it here. The poem was widely read on the social media and a fellow known as Best Agbese, who is a doctoral student at the University of Dundee, wrote a rendition of the poem. Permit me to reproduce the poem and Agbese's rendition as well:

ARE YOU A TERRORIST?

Living in the jungle or in the city?
In the market place or in the park?
Roaming the city streets or the bush paths?
Breaking terror news from a reporter

Or breaking hearts in the worship places?
Are you a terrorist?
Who believes all others not of him are lost?
Or he who believes those who fight
In defence of citizens have no faith?
A cause and a patriotic faith they have.

Are you a terrorist?
Who sees only one course to his ascendancy
Or who provides many reasons to blame
Those patriots that daily sacrifice for the nation?

Are you a terrorist?
Who remains mute when the enemy strikes
The innocent but blames the patriotic
Forces without offering any civic hand?

Are you a terrorist?
Who supports the enemy's propaganda
Or who attacks the patriots' genuine
psychological operations
Or who condemns policies toward solutions?

Are you a terrorist?
Who is quick to spread the fake news?
Spread any adverse news on the patriots?
Or who always finds faults of the patriots
In the fields or in their abodes.
Be a patriot and never a terrorist.

Now, the rendition of the poem:

WHY I WILL BE A PATRIOT, NOT A TERRORIST!

Rendition of a poem by Best Agbese

The COAS, Lt. Gen. TY Buratai, is a bundle of talents. A famed soldier, he is also a consummate and prolific poet. General Buratai selects his poetic themes carefully and dwells on very touchy contemporary issues. He infuses into his poetry very powerful emotions while crafting his thoughts.

In a poetic piece titled "Are You A Terrorist?" General Buratai examined the wretched, rustic life of a terrorist. He identifies actions or concealed inactions of seeming onlookers which bear trademarks of terrorism.

In the opening stanza, the poet begins with a series of rhetorical questions. He presents and compares two general lifestyles at the disposal of the terrorist. One portrays the beauty of an alluring life in a normal world a terrorist denies himself. He contrasts it with

The author of *The Legend of Buratai Volume One* donating 200 copies of the book to the principal of FGC, Jos after the book reading.

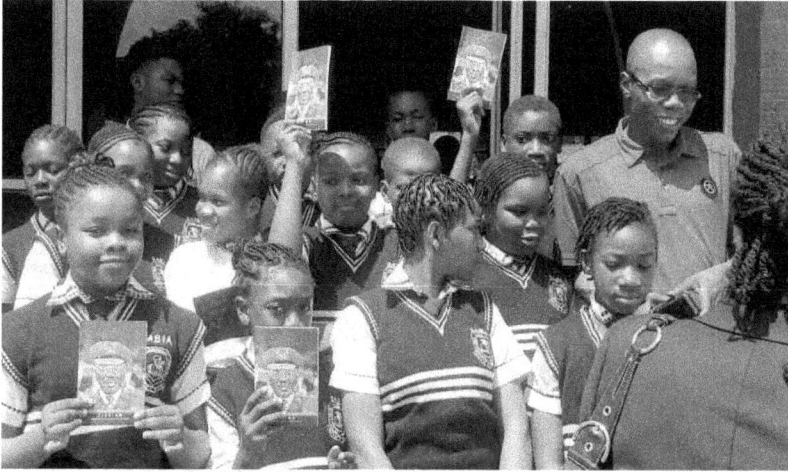

Students of Bill and Samuel School, Abuja and the author of *The Legend of Buratai Volume One* when Sprezzatura Publishing organized a book reading at the school.

the ignoble beast-like and lonely life he imposes on himself by living with chirruping birds and dangerous reptiles in forests, caves and mountains, perpetually dreading his shadows.

He writes: "Living in the jungle or in the city?" The city in everyday life embodies all the niceties and comfort life can offer. In this realm of normality, there are limitless opportunities of comfort and a prosperous life for the individual.

And the next line again asks the terrorists whether he prefers a squalid life, "In the market place or in the park? Roaming the city streets or the bush paths?"

While the poet portrays two worlds, the stanza intimates that the terrorist foists on himself a life of squalor and misery, even when he kisses the city gates. He is a tout for choosing the life of blood and destructions and so, denies himself of the goodies of existence.

Audu and Baruk presenting a souvenir to me when we hosted
school children at the Army Headquarters in Abuja.

The poet proceeds to mock the terrorist's imposition
of deprivations on himself. He writes; "Breaking
terror news from a reporter;" because a terrorist is the
harbinger of bad news; he pleasures in propagating
gory pictures of victims of his sadism.

The poet sermonizes that a terrorist is very scared of
breaking his own news freely like other normal human
beings. This in itself alludes to his mental derangement.

It is explicable because he is cursed by a cruel fate. That terrorists also deprive themselves of the pleasures life offers by satanic wickedness is alluded to in this verse: "Or breaking hearts in the worship places?" Even in sacred places, they exhibit their satanism.

And in the third stanza, the poet parodies the convictions of the terrorist, as he says; "Are you a terrorist?" He continues by challenging the guts and might of a terrorist who swims in false illusion about

The retired Major General Penap receiving a souvenir at Port Harcourt during the presentation of *The Legend of Buratai Volume One*.

Students at Kirikasama UBE School, seating under the tree while the classes are being renovated by a good Samaritan

Public presentation and reading of *The Legend of Buratai, Volume 1* to students at the Federal Government College, Jos in October 2019.

Students of Mafoni Liberty UBE School, Maiduguri in a group photograph with the author and the school management after the book reading of "The Legend of Buratai, Volume 1".

the defeat of humanity by atrocious acts. He says a terrorist is an imbecile and feeble-minded: "Who believes all others not of him are lost? /Or he who believes those who fight."

And the poet suggests reassuringly that a terrorist erroneously believes troops who battle them in trenches, "In defence of citizens have no faith?", A cause and a patriotic faith they have." Now, the poet goes into outright deriding of terrorists, who in the mindset of the poet are paperweights in the battles they start.

In the next stanza, the poet comes out more forcefully against terrorists' misconceptions and ideological bent. Permanently relying on the style of repetition, he again asks; "Are you a terrorist?" The poet thinks terrorists are effeminate warriors who are barren of valour to face real gallant men like Nigerian troops on the battlefield. Rather they sneak out in the dead of the night to unleash violence on helpless women, children and their aged parents, only to lay false claims to bravery. But they are nothing other than cowards who scamper at the sight of battle with troops too many times.

The poet explains further that the terrorist is a cursed fighter "Who sees only one course to his ascendancy/ Or who provides many reasons to blame/Those patriots that daily sacrifice for the nation?"

Having drenched the soul of the terrorists in acerbic tirades and invectives, he migrates to innuendic allusion to sympathisers and agents of terrorists. Searching their ungodly souls, the poet descends heavily on the dead consciences of this set of other children of Adam and Eve obviously under a curse.

He asks, "Are you a terrorist?" who remains mute when the enemy strikes the innocent but blames the patriotic forces without offering any civic hand?

Terrorists' agents and sympathisers who display pretentious empathy for the nation under the spell of terrorism expose themselves wittingly. According to the poet, their antics are not only known, but the

Myself and some senior Army officers at Limankara when the COAS visited the MOPOL Training base in December 2019. Third from left is Major General Adebayo and next to him is Major General Angbazo.

message is conveyed very poignantly by their silence in the face of action to appease the wailing blood of the innocent crying for justice.

The poet campaigner is saying it is absolutely nonsensical to blame troops when Boko Haram accomplices either cleverly encourage terrorism by reneging to enlist in the fight or project a perforated sense of patriotism.

There is a lengthy scolding of disparate categories of veiled shadowy existence of terrorists in many subsisting subsets who pose as saints. While the poet tries as much as possible not to offend their sensibilities, he repeats the same question: "Are you a terrorist?" And he provides answers, an indication from the answers that terrorist sympathisers function in a wild range, which include those "Who supports the enemy's propaganda/ Or who attacks the patriots' genuine psychological operations/Or who condemns policies toward solutions?"

Perusing the poet's mind, it connotes that a terrorist includes that politician who kicks against Government policies designed to end terrorism or the cronies he recruits for this purpose. They include the formal and informal pen pushers who hype or celebrate terrorists' publicity stunts. They are all guilty of cyberspace terrorism, the poet mutters mildly.

Mr. Best Agbese, a PhD student of The University of Dundee who wrote the rendition of the poem "Are You A Terrorist?"

The next stanza explains it more pungently and heartily. In the last phase of the repetition, "Are You A Terrorist?", the poet punctures this issue which obsesses his mind all day and every minute, as he crafts the poem. He thunders condescendingly and condemnably on allies of terrorists. The poem asks unreservedly and asserts that by your actions, you have affinity with terrorists if you are the personality, "Who is quick to spread the fake news?" Or the type who is eager to "Spread any adverse news on the patriots?" Or who always finds faults of the patriots/ In the fields or in their abodes."

The overriding preoccupation of the poet is to examine the operative nuances of terrorists and terrorism. Through a unique poetic style of repetition, an impressive use of the stream of consciousness and mastery of diction, he finely conveys a contemporary message on terrorism which pierces every heart.

The poet fruitfully counsels all not only to resent terrorists and abhor terrorism, but always to be a patriot and never a terrorist.

Agbese, a patriot and PhD student at University of Dundee, wrote from Scotland:

This poem, I must say, is a strategic tool for countering violence extremism which leads to terrorism (CVELT). Insurgents are usually indoctrinated through violent and/or extremists' ideologies which eventually lead them to employ terrorism because of their cowardice and incompetence. I am sure that some of them will read this poem and its rendition and eventually have a rethink. Not only to have a rethink but to head the clarion call of becoming a patriot and shunning terrorism in all its ramifications

☙ LESSON ❧

Nigeria's call to all of us who are supposed to be compatriots is to serve her with love, strength and faith so that the labour of our past heroes (Herbert Macaulay, Sir Ahmadu Bello, Chief Obafemi Awolowo. Nnamdi Azikiwe, General Murtala Mohammed etc.) will not be in vain. Let me say categorically that we are called to serve Nigeria by displaying three things: love towards one another, strength and courage, and lastly faith in God. If we stick to Nigeria's call as it is clearly spelt out in the National Anthem, we will shun terrorism and remain patriots.

*"If your actions inspire others
to dream more, learn more,
do more and become more,
you are a leader."*

John Quincy Adams

CHAPTER FIFTEEN

❖ ❖ ❖

Yamtarawala, the Great King and warrior

Yamtarawala was first of all the great prince who founded the Biu Royal Dynasty. His mother was a beautiful woman, known as Asga, who got married to the King of Ngazargamu of the Kanem Borno Empire. Ngazargamu is not far from present-day Gaidam, which is located in Yobe State, Nigeria. She had two sons for the King, but some courtiers were not sure of the paternity of the first child, whose name was Abdullahi. Even though they kept this matter close to their chest, they made it a serious matter after the King died. They told Abdullahi: "We cannot ascertain the veracity or otherwise of your paternity to the King. What we believe is that your mother, Queen Asga, was pregnant with you when she married your father. You might be the son of the King of Yemen. For this reason, we will anoint Ahmed your brother as king."

Abdullahi was furious. "How dare you!" he roared. "You kept mum and refused to discuss this matter when my father was alive because your intentions were not honourable. Now that he is dead, you want to sow the seed of discord between me and my brother and deprive me of my inheritance."

"No, don't say that, Abdullahi," said one of the kingmakers. "We have to do what is right to preserve the king's bloodline."

"Listen and listen to me very well. I don't care about what you say or what you think. I will be king, God willing. I am destined to be king. By God, you shall see that one day I am king. All of you."

Abdullahi was furious and he immediately made up his mind to leave Ngazargamu town. He took all the weapons he could lay his hands on and summoned his loyalists and supporters to leave the town. He couldn't stand the sight of seeing his younger brother as king and lord over him. It was a tense moment for the kingdom.

Abdullahi went away with a total of seventy men and their families. They headed to Biu land, where the Bura people and others like the Tera, Kanakuru and Fulbe were sojourning. At that time, there was no king in Biu land. The people lived in clusters of clan villages protected by village stone walls, which they called *michiba* in the Babur Bura language. Each village was independent of the others. Buratai was on its own. So also were Miringa, Mandaragrau and so on. There were no royal families, as each village was headed by someone referred to as *mthlakurdi*, which in the English tongue means lord of the land.

The people occupying the land of Biu before Abdullahi, who later became known as Yamtarawala, migrated to Biu around 1000 AD from the east. Yamtarawala settled in a village known as Limbur. He found Bura people in the villages of Miringa, Mandaragrau, Buratai and Diwas. Because of his superior military prowess, he was able to defeat and conquer all the villages except Buratai. He did so through military superiority and sometimes through marital alliances. It might be of interest to know that the descendants of Ahmed, Yamtarawala's brother, are no longer the custodians of the Kanem Borno stool. They were out-manoeuvred and upstaged by a great scholar cum military tactician known as Muhammad al Amin al Kanemi, who was half Berber Arab and half Kanembu.

The name 'Yamtarawala' is a conundrum in itself because of the numerous versions and dimensions it has. I should like to say that there are about five different versions of the meaning of Yamtarawala of Biu. First of all, there is the school of thought that said the name was derived from the phrase, "Ngza Yamta kisi laburtsa-Yamta naawaltsa!" which when translated means, "See, another Yamta had come for us, the bigger Yamta!"

It was reported that the people of Biu used to have a noble hero known as Yamta, who died. His death brought great sadness to the land of Biu because he was a good man, so it was with great relief that they welcomed the new immigrant to their land. This was why everyone in the land was saying another Yamta had come. Some people said that the name Yamtarawala was given to him because of his link with the old Yamta.

The second version said that the name was derived from the Arabic phrase "Youman tarakawallahi," which when translated into English means "I will be the leader of the people." It was said that Yamtarawala uttered these words when he lost out in the chieftaincy contest between himself and his younger brother.

There is another school of thought that said Yamtarawala derived his name from the word "Chief" when he cried, "Youman-teram-wallahi ana sultan insha Allah," which in English means "One day you shall see that I am a Chief, God willing."

There is yet another version that said Yamtarawala got his name from his mother. She said, "Yamta Ula, I have seen a vision that you will leave Borno and go to Viu (Biu) to become king." His mother was known as Asga, but is it not certain whether Mai Idriss Katagarmabe or Mai Idris Aloma was his father.

The last version, which says Yamtarawala got his name when he told the daughter of the Chief of Miringa, Kwatam Gambo "Yauma tara wala," is more romantic and sensational.

Kwatam Gambo was the daughter of the local chief, and she helped Yamtarawala and led him to the water point at the local shrine of Miringa. Yamtarawala had asked her to help him to locate the site of the shrine so that he could eventually take control of the town. Yamtarawala had a strategy of defeating and taking control of towns through subterfuge and subtlety and not just through warfare alone. In Mandaragrau,

Miringa, and Diwa, he befriended the chief's daughter, who eventually gave him the secret of defeating the town. According to this version, when some people in the community asked Kwatam about the identity of the man she was mingling with, she said the man simply told her that he was "Yomutarawala," and it was from there that the people started referring to him as "Yamtarawala."

He was a very wise man who knew how to plan and achieve his goal. When he arrived at Mandaragrau, he waited patiently for the right time to strike. He befriended the chief's daughter, married her and asked her to reveal to him the secret behind the security of Mandaragrau. Upon obtaining the secret, he seized control of the town. In Miringa, he did the same. It wasn't so easy because Miringa was well fortified by its Mumba charm, which was hidden inside its shrine, but again he married the chief's daughter, who later revealed the secret to him. He performed the required rituals and thereafter took control of the shrine. This made the people voluntarily submit to him. He did the same thing in the village of Diwa. The sad thing there was that he returned to Diwa and killed everyone, including the chief's daughter who had revealed the secret to him.

In 1560, something horrible happened in the family of Yamtarawala. He was a mystical man and very powerful, to the extent that his subjects viewed him as superhuman. Yamtarawala, who had six children, wanted to test them to see if any of them possessed spiritual powers like him. He took a piece of stone, put it in water in a pot and placed it on the fire. He allowed it to boil for some time before calling on the children to come and check if the stone was cooked. One after the other, they checked it and said, "Long live the Kuthli, the stone is not cooked; it is still as hard as a rock can be." But Marivirahyel, his first son, did the unthinkable. He used the small stick his father gave them to check if the stone was cooked and pierced the stone. He lifted it out of the pot, grabbed it with his hands and began to eat it. He didn't stop there but went on to say "The stone is well cooked," as he tore it with his teeth.

Apart from the fact that this development meant that Marivirahyel possessed higher powers than his father, because only a higher power can make a stone soft, it was clearly an insult. The great Yamtarawala was not someone who could stand this kind of insult, because he attached so much importance to his respect and dignity. He was someone who wanted to be feared and dreaded by all and sundry but alas, someone born in his own house was testing his patience.

Yamtarawala was furious. He withdrew into his shell and became unusually quiet. After this, some members of his council advised him to kill the rebellious prince. The prince suspected that he might be killed by his father, so he fled the town in the night. When the assassins came to execute him, he was nowhere to be found. The messengers of death were afraid to tell Yamtarawala that Marivirahyel had escaped, so they told him he was dead.

After this, people began to come to the King to pay their condolences. A group of people visiting the King had the shock of their lives when they encountered Marivirahyel on the road. The young prince mocked them and said, "If you meet my father, the great King, tell him that I, Mari, am still alive and well. In fact, tell him that if he has *fura*, I have *nono* and if he has *nono*, I have *fura*. If he is not comfortable with this offer tell him that if he has taba (tobacco), I have *kilbu*."

This was a direct challenge from a son to his father. Yamtarawala was furious upon hearing the bad news, so he cursed the bearers of it. He was angry with those who had told him that Marivirahyel was dead, because the whole thing had now become a joke. He sent everyone out of the palace.

"I want to be alone," he said. He sat on his throne alone and was contemplating the matter. "How in the world did Mari's powers cook my stone? What will I do with this rebellious son of mine who is now aware that I sent people to kill him? How will my subjects look at me now? Isn't it ridiculous to be described as a king who tried to have his rebellious son killed but failed? In the first place, it is wrong for a king to kill his son, but had I succeeded, I could have been feared. But to fail in this small task is a great shame."

Yamtarawala was the kind of individual who believed that a life without honour and respect was not worth living. As he sat on his throne, boiling with rage, something strange began to happen. The great Yamtarawala began to sink into the ground beneath him.

When her feminine instinct told her that something was wrong, his favourite daughter decided to go and see him. All she could see was the top of his head, as the remaining parts of his body were all beneath the earth. But before his head could vanish into the ground, she took a sharp knife and cut off his pigtail. The piece of hair that she cut off is now known as the *zukumbli* and it is now a symbol of authority for every king of Biu.

Yamtarawala, the founder of the Biu chiefdom, was succeeded by Kuthli Vira Hyel, who reigned from 1560 to 1565 AD, after which Kuthli Dawi-Rawala, the third king of the realm, reigned from 1565 to 1606 AD, making him the second longest ruler of Biu. He reigned for forty years. The fourth ruler of Biu was Kuthli Yamta Amba who reigned from 1605 to 1635 AD, after which Kuthli Yamta Kupaya Wadi reigned from 1635 to 1670 AD. The sixth chief was Mari Watila Tamta, who ruled for ten years and was succeeded by Kuthli Luku Yamtara Banye. Kuthli Banye reigned from 1680 to 1690 AD, after which his son Kuthli Luku reigned for another ten years and died in 1700 AD. The ninth king was Mai Birtitik, who also ruled for ten years. After him were Mai Mari Thama Bahara, Mai Mari Tayar Warinki, Mai Dakwai, Mai Mari Kopachi, Mai Diporma, Mai Garga Mwada, Mai Dimoda Dawimoda and Mai Dibiya.

One thing that is special about these kings is their length of reign; from Mai Watila Tamta all through to Mai Dibiya, all ruled Biu for a period of ten years each. Two among these kings, Garga Moda and Garga Kopchi, were killed by the Fulani invaders in 1770 and 1793 AD respectively. After them came the short-lived reign of the chiefdom, for Mai Dirawa ruled for only three years and died in 1803 AD. He was succeeded by Mai Garga Kupachi in 1803 who also ruled for ten years. After him was Mai Mari Watirwam, who ruled for forty-five years. He was the longest serving monarch of the realm. He was the great king of Biu who foiled the attacks of Mai Buba Yero of Gombe when the Fulani invaders decided to attack and overran Biu. Mai Mari Watirwam was a great warrior. He led his royal army to defeat the invaders without any external help or support.

Mai Ali Paskur succeeded him and ruled for thirty-five years. Then came Mai Mari Biya, who ruled for eight years and was succeeded by Mai Garga Kwanting, who ruled for a brief period of seven years. Then one of the greatest and most charismatic rulers of Biu appeared on the scene as king and reigned for thirty-three years. His name was Mai Ali Dogo. He was succeeded by Mai Ali Gurgur, who reigned from 1935 to 1951. He was succeeded by Mai Muhammadu Aliyu, who ruled for eight years. He died exactly a year before I was born in Buratai. He was succeeded by Mai Mustapha Aliyu in 1959 as the twenty-seventh king of Biu. Mai Aliyu reigned for thirty years before he was succeeded by Mai Umar Mustapha in 1989.

I should like to say that the authentic name of the Babur ethnic nationality is Pabir, which according to J.G Davies, who authored a book titled Biu Book, are a mixture of Bura clans, other tribes in the area and those who immigrated from Ngazagamu with Yamtarawala.

Yamtarawala established his Kingdom in the area and ruled from 1535 to 1560. There used to be a separate kingdom in Mandiragrau because Yamtarawala's kingdom was split into Mandaragirau, Gongdi, and Yimirdalang (Davies,1954) but it was two important dynasties that sprang up after his death: the Kogu, which is in Biu, and Mandaragirau, which was founded by Ali Sokar, son of the 12th Babur Chief Mai Dawi and a brother of the 13th Biu Chief Mari Kwopchi in 1740. It became a separate kingdom helping the Babur in war but not subservient to it". There was a time when the Mandaragirau chiefdom was independent of Biu, but the latter seized to be independent in 1911 when Mai Mari was deposed by the District Officer, Mr JHC Eider. Mandaragirau first came into the limelight because of a disagreement between two brothers, during the reign of the 12th kuthli, or king, who was known as Mai Dawi. His oldest son and heir apparent to the throne, Ali Sokar went to war against some intruders (possibly Fulani) but unfortunately for him his father, the king, died in his absence. The Crown Prince was shocked to discover after his return that his younger brother, Mari Kopchi, had taken over the throne as king. Ali Sokar became so upset and angry that he shouted saying "Wan viri" in Babur language. In English, "Wan viri" means "Who installed" his brother and it was from there that Woviri ruling clan derived their name.

From 1740 in the Biu area there were the kingdoms of Babur, Mandaragirau, Shani, Shelleng and some other village kingdoms like Kwaya Tera, Yimirdllang, Walama and Gusi. The Babur kingdom, which was rightfully controlled by Garga Kwamting when he was made Chief of Babur (Biu) in 1904, consisted of the present village areas of Biu, Gur, Gunda, Garubula, Miringa, Buratai, Kida, Kwaya Bura, Hyema, Vina and Zira. The Dagil clan is the clan of the Chief of Mandaragirau. They are the main clans of Babur who came with Yamtarawala like the Woviri clan. Davies stated that the Dagil clan members were found in Mandaragirau, Viyukamda (Biu), Virahyel and Ngonga (Kida). The headquarters of the Dagil Kingdom was moved to the present Mandaragirau town probably towards the middle of the 18th century when the Chief defeated the original inhabitants of the Bwala clan and made one of them Thlerima (Galadima). For a full detail of the lineage foundation of the two kingdoms, that is Biu and Mandaragirau, see Appendix C.

The present king of Biu is Mai Mustapha, who has been occupying the throne for thirty years now. Just like the legendary Yamtarawala, the people of Biu and their kings have always been fearless, independent-minded and courageous. When the Boko Haram insurgents terrorised and sacked many towns and chiefdoms in the north-east, the King of Biu and his subjects refused to run to safety like the other kings who fled, surrendering their towns and domains to the insurgents. The King or Mai of Biu stood his ground, rallied his people and defended his honour like a king. His courage was superbly regal, and this feat earned him enormous respect from his subjects.

Yamtarawala will forever be remembered as a great military commander, king, ruler and statesman. The stories of people like Alexander the Great, Iliya Dan Maikarfi and General Maimalari inspired me as a youth, but that of Yamtarawala is something else because I can easily relate to him. Both of us came from the same area and have the same physique and stature, both of us are military commanders, both of us like hunting and hate injustice, and both of us are loyal to constituted authority. The only difference is that my family doesn't have royal blood like his, so we have no interest in ruling people. We serve the realm. There exists a cordial relationship between me and his dynasty. I intend to keep it that way through my unflinching loyalty.

Yamtarawala, the great king and warrior

∾ LESSON ∾

The basic lesson we can learn from the life and times of Yamtarawala is fearlessness and courage. He was simply a no-nonsense man who refused to surrender his destiny to the control of the whims and caprices of others. It is also good to note that he knew how and when to compromise, and he also showed us that it is not good for one to fight his own kin because of power. Though he was stronger, he refused to confront his brother; instead he left them to start fresh somewhere else. Yamtarawala believed that power comes from God and God has a thousand and one ways to actualize his dreams. If you are meant to be a king, a ruler or a leader among people, God will by all means make it happen so long as you remain resolute and work towards harmony.

"Soldiers, when committed to a task, can't compromise. It's unrelenting devotion to the standards of duty and courage, absolute loyalty to others, not letting the task go until it's been done."

John Keegan

CHAPTER SIXTEEN

❖ ❖ ❖

PrInCIPLes

1. Don't bother about what people say – they are entitled to their own opinion and there is no way everyone will agree with you. The time you spend bothering about what is said about you could have been productively used to achieve other things that would add value to your life. Though we are more similar than we are different, we happen to be different where it matters the most. A disagreement is not a denial of your worth, but a reflection of the other person's understanding and personage.

2. Commit to improving yourself to the extent that you don't have time to compete or criticize others. Being true to yourself is the ability to beam the light of criticism inward, and use it as a catalyst for growth and improvement. You will always live with yourself for the rest of your life; therefore, spend time to compete with yourself in the form of

setting goals and trying to achieve them. To truly "compete" with another is impossible. How do you compete when you are different people motivated by different things, with different desires? Focus on your own path.

3. Let excellence be your trademark anywhere you find yourself; avoid mediocrity at all costs. Excellence and mediocrity cannot co-exist; if one stays the other leaves, and you are solely responsible for the choice you make in this case. At the end of it all, it is what drives you in life that would also motivate the road you choose. And all I know is that excellence has never failed. See mediocrity as an enemy. You should never be found unarmed in the camp of an enemy.

4. Don't be too proud to retrace your steps back to the right path if you discovered that you are on the wrong path. Mistakes are part of life. Anytime you find you have made one, it is great wisdom to seek redress. Pride has caused more harm than good in our world today. Where pride cannot go, humility can. Try not to always see yourself as too important so that you can have the freedom to learn how to help yourself towards a more fulfilling existence.

5. Listen more and say less. Instead talk loud with your actions. There is time for everything; knowing when and how to use your tongue would save you from a lot of many calamities. God has given us two ears as a sign that we need to listen more. Words can be powerful, but actions are much more powerful.

6. Always lead with courage, or not at all. Leadership is not luxury. It is even more challenging when you are in the battlefield of life. However, if you become a leader where all has been entrusted to your care, you have no choice but to lead with total bravery. Always trust your guts; you can do it if you decide!

7. Honour your word as your bond and never make a promise you can't keep. This is a great mark of integrity. This is where an absolute control of your emotions comes into play. Always know what to give and what to keep. The little promise you fulfil makes you more honourable than the many you promised just to get adulation from the crowd.

8. Don't expect everybody to understand you because you must have seen the light in the horizon before them as a leader. It is the duty of the leader to motivate his/her followers, especially when they don't seem to be enjoying the journey towards a goal. Patience is key and being decisive is a necessity when the need arises. When the team's morale is down, the leader must awake to build new strategies for the way forward.

9. Beware of flattery. Surround yourself with those who will tell you the truth, for this may turn out to your advantage in the long run. On the other hand, flattery puffs you up temporarily and leaves you flattened afterwards.

10. Always try to be fair, but don't compromise your standards. Taking others into consideration is a great way to live your life; however, when you forget who you are in the attempt to please others, you become a fool of your own making. In all, know when to draw the line and all will be fine.

11. Read good books, but also learn how to read people. Sometimes, the books you read show you the different people you know or have around you. The idea of knowing the other person is to help you determine the quality of interaction you have with people. Knowledge is vital to succeed in life.

12. Don't allow anyone or anything to disturb your peace and make you lose control of your mind. In your mind is where you should dwell all the time, because that is where every one of your external actions stems from. Therefore, let it remain prohibited to intruders; those with bitter taste about life. Don't dwell there in idleness but in constant renewal of the self.

13. Always remember that time is precious, that your life itself is a measure of time, so make every minute count. By the time you finish reading this, some seconds must have gone by. Plan your time; don't allow time to plan you. There are 24 hours in a day for everybody, but some make better use of theirs than others.

14. Honour and respect womanhood. This is where the whole of humanity revolves. A woman is the 'tree of life'. You need her in your life as a man, and we need her as a nation.

15. Always make peace with your conscience and do the right thing because it is right. Believe in what you do, even if no one else does You are the best example of yourself. And no one, I mean no one, can do it better than you. Never doubt your conscience because it is where you find yourself; if you have a bad one, you should never trust your conscience.

16. Give your superiors and your associates 100% loyalty. Loyalty is non-negotiable in building camaraderie. Your superior needs your loyalty as much as you need his/her leadership. In the end, it pays for all parties.

17. Never underrate or undervalue yourself. Your worth can only be proven by you, so learn to rise above your inferiority complex.

18. Stay positive and clean in thoughts and in your appearance. Every well-refined thought has the potential of creating something beautiful. Always present yourself in the most positive way you can.

19. Honour the elders, especially your father and mother. Respect for one's elders can never go out of date. As Africans, this is a strong value for us to take as ours and to live with all the days of our

lives, no matter where we find ourselves on the face of the Earth. Giving respect to elders is priceless, and is a sign of a well- trained individual. It also shows that one is ready to become a respectable elder someday. More so as our parents are the tools God has used to give us life. We are all the time indebted to them and owe them our deep respect.

∽ LESSON ∽

These then are my life guiding principles, and if you want to excel and succeed in life as a military officer or any kind of leader, I believe they will be of tremendous help to you.

POSTCRIPT

❖ ❖ ❖

BY Dr ABUBAKar MOHAMMED sani

I must now explain the reason I decided to collaborate with General Buratai, the legend, to write this book. First of all, I truly believe that his exploits and gallantry are legendary and therefore worth documenting in a format that youngsters and students can read and derive inspiration from. Secondly, and this is most dear to my heart, my son Audu loves and adores the COAS to such an extent that whenever and wherever he sees his image, he goes wild with joy. "Daddy, see General. I want to be like him. He is my friend," he will say.

While Volume One of this book was single-handedly written by myself, this second volume was a joint effort between myself and General Buratai. In fact, the bulk of the work was borne by General Buratai, who conceived the idea, nurtured it and provided the stories that made the book what it is. I must say that the willingness of General Buratai to spend long hours of the night narrating stories of past events, and his diligence in seeing that everything was done meticulously, still amaze me. There were nights when we stayed awake until 1 am in the Theatre Command. General Buratai's ability to move around army bases and formations across the theatre from eight in the morning through to eight in the evening, wash, meet with his lieutenants for briefings and still go on with this book, made me fully loyal to him and also strengthened my belief in his leadership, professionalism and generalship. I am still of the opinion that he is the best General Africa has produced in the last decade.

Writing, editing and critiquing this book with General Buratai made me see the other side of the man. He is not just an infantry General but also a historian and a lover of children and animals. He also has a special interest in paranormal activities. Beyond that, he has a very down-to-earth personality and is unusually calm and unperturbed. He radiates the aura of a true legend, and I think there is something extraordinary about the man. I have interviewed and interacted with his schoolmates and NDA course mates. I have also interacted with family and traditional historians and chiefs in Biu and Buratai. What I heard was awesome. I don't think he has changed that much. He is always calm, cool and collected. He thinks a lot. He doesn't get into unnecessary fights. He talks a little and listens very much. He loves sports and has a strong faith in God and destiny. He is always neat and diligent and knows how best to manage human resources. He is a true soldier, and he believes that just like Rommel, Montgomery and Patton, he has a special calling to be an infantry General.

I must say that I consider it a rare privilege to have the opportunity to sit down with the nation's Chief of Army Staff and collaborate to produce this second volume. I shall forever remain grateful that my child, and many other children out there, can now have something to serve as a moral compass and motivation to excel in their studies and life's ambition. I feel this book will make it easy for a child to know and appreciate what he needs to do to become a General. For those youngsters who don't have a passion for the Army, the life principles of General Buratai—diligence, excellence, loyalty, hard work, patience, endurance, honesty, courage and faith in God—are all they need to succeed in any endeavour they will choose. These principles were what made the man stand out from the crowd, and I am yet to see anybody who exhibited these virtues who is not great.

APPENDICES

❖ ❖ ❖

APPENDIX A

STAGES OF MY PROMOTION WITH DATES

Lieutenant (January 1985)

Captain (January 1989)

Major (January 1994)

Lieutenant Colonel (January 1998)

Colonel (January 2004)

Brigadier General (January 2009)

Major General (January 2012)

Lieutenant General (August 2015)

LT GEN TY BURATAI HONOURS AND AWARDS:

The COAS Following Honours and Awards:

- Nigerian Army Medal (NAM),

- Order of Military Merit (OMM (BR))
- Forces Service Star (FSS),
- Meritorious Service Star (MSS),
- Distinguished Service Star (DSS)
- Grand Service Star (GSS).
- Pass Staff Course Dagger (psc(+)),
- National Defence College (ndc (BD)),
- Field Command Medal of Honour (FCMH),
- Foreign National Honours Award Medal (FNHAM),
- Training Support Medal (TSM)
- United Nations Medal for Angolan Verification Medal II (UNAVEM
- Masters of Arts Degree in History (BA Hons)
- Master of Philosophy Degree in Security Studies (MA Mphil),
- Honorary Doctorate Degree in Leadership and Peace (PhD).
- Training Support Medal
- United Nations Medal for Angolan Verification Medal II.
- Northeast Star Magazine's Man of the Year, 2016
- Brazilian Military Order of Merit Award,2017
- The Politico Magazine's Man of the Year,2017
- The Millennium Achiever, 2018 by The Nigerian News, London

- Northeast Star Magazine's Colin Powell Meritorious Award for
- Soldering of the Decade (2008-2018)
- Leadership Newspaper's Exemplary and Uncommon

  Leadership Command Award, 2018
- The Tribune's Man of the Year, 2018
- Institute of Management Technology, Enugu's SUG 2018

  Leadership Award for being the Most Proactive COAS in

  Nigeria's recent history
- Presidential Award for Excellence, 2018
- Most Outstanding COAS, 2020 by The Society Watch Magazine
- The Nigerian News' Most Outstanding Legend of the Year, 2020
- Man of the Year 2020, Daily Asset Newspaper

APPENDIX B

❖ ❖ ❖

INSURGENCY AND TERRORISM: WHY THE COAS DESERVE COMMENDATIONS

By Abubakar MS

I have been an avid reader of the biography of gallant and valiant military generals all over the world. I will always remain fascinated by the lifestyle, leadership, and patriotism of men like An-Nasir Salah ad-Din Yusuf ibn Ayyub, known as Salah ad-Din or Saladin, Napoleon Bonaparte, Dwight D. Eisenhower, Douglas MacArthur, Collin Powell, Brigadier Zakariya Maimalari and a host of others.

Here in Nigeria, I have taken time to study and reflect on the military and this is why I have taken a special interest on the person of Lt. General Tukur Yusufu Buratai, the 20th Chief of Army Staff of the Nigerian Army which to mind is the most potent institution that has been able to keep this fragile country of ours as one indivisible entity in peace. The purpose of this paper is to examine and analyze the achievements of the Nigeria Army in its fight against

Boko Haram terrorists from 2015 to date. I am writing this article from two different perspectives. First of all, I am talking from the perspective of someone who was born and raised in the North-East, and secondly from the perspective of a media professional who has

been able to interact with key stakeholders and the masses in the North-East. I make bold to say that there is a consensus in the North-East that General Buratai's leadership of the Army has been superb although I understand that some people disagree with that. And this minority is gradually becoming very vocal by the day possibly because of the hit and run attacks the insurgents were able to carry out in the northeast. Let me say, categorically, that this essay is concerned with the North-East region only and even here it is vis-à-vis the Boko Haram security challenge.

Although Boko Haram insurgency which was started by the late Muhammad Yusuf became violent and deadly in 2011, the vicious sect became renowned for wanton destruction of lives and property beginning from 2013 and it reaches its peak between 2014 to early 2015. The US Government's publication, A Guide to the Analysis of Insurgency defines Insurgency as "a protracted political-military struggle directed toward subverting or displacing the legitimacy of a constituted government or occupying power and completely or partially controlling the resources of a territory through the use of irregular military forces and illegal political organizations. The common denominator for most insurgent groups is their objective of gaining control of a population or a particular territory, including its resources. This objective differentiates insurgent groups from purely terrorist organizations." Boko Haram terrorists became famous through beheading, kidnap of schoolgirls, suicide bombings, and attack of a military base in the North-East region of Nigeria. Bamidele (2015) pointed out that the Boko Haram insurgency was "exacerbated by weak governance."

The state failed to provide necessities has aggravated socio-economic grievances which have in turn been exploited by terrorist groups such as Boko Haram terrorists." Despite the efforts of the previous government of President Goodluck Jonathan, Boko Haram continued to unleash havoc on Nigerian soil to the extent of sacking and seizing numerous towns (Bamidele, p.12. 2015).

While it is true that Boko Haram and/or ISWAP insurgency that Nigeria is confronted with is receiving tacit international support from the war entrepreneurs and enemies of Nigeria, we should be bold enough to tell ourselves to the bitter truth that our collective actions and in-actions as a nation created the fertile ground needed for the insurgents to operate. The political leadership of Borno state made the mistake of lionizing the late Muhammad Yusuf when the leaders of the All Nigeria Peoples Party (ANPP) contacted him for support to win the 2003 gubernatorial elections. This acknowledgment and glorification of Yusuf was further re-enforced when one of his protégé was offered the position of commissioner in the administration of Senator Ali Modu Sheriff. The estranged union between Senator Sheriff and the sect collapsed and sowed the seed of discord between the two partners and it was said that public sympathy was with the sect after they pulled out of the government which they labeled corrupt. Added to this was the failure of the government at both the state and federal levels to provide the "basic services, such as security, justice, health care, education, utilities, or transportation infrastructure." This situation was further compounded by inept security forces, especially the police because they interact most frequently with the people. Then, lastly, a window of vulnerability was created when the police killed some of the sect's members for refusing to put on crash helmets which later culminated in the extermination of Muhammad Yusuf. After that, the insurgency took a violent turn.

The Nigerian military especially the Army had done a lot in combating Boko Haram insurgency since its inception in 2009 but according to Omeni (2017), the assumption of the present crop of service chiefs especially the Chief of Army Staff (COAS), General Buratai led to the rapid decline of the terrorist group in Nigeria because of his bravery, strategic leadership, and superior skills in tactics. When General Buratai came on board as COAS, nineteen local government areas across three states (Borno, Adamawa, and Yobe) were under the firm control of the insurgents where they were able to suspend the constitution and enforce their version of the sharia. But General Buratai, like

General Ulysses Grant, relocated to the theatre of operations to take charge of the war and within six months defeated the insurgents and reclaimed all the nineteen local governments that were hitherto under the control of the insurgents. It was after that they all moved to a suitable terrain to hide and continued to come out to launch hit and run attacks. The Nigerian Army pursued the insurgents into the Sambisa forest, decimated them, and took over the critical base like Camp Zairo. Even though a remnant of the insurgents are still carrying out hit and run attacks, Mahmoud and Ani (2018) emphasized that "the areas where both factions of Boko Haram have been active are peripheral regions within the countries in which they sit (North-East Nigeria, Diffa region of Niger, Far North province in Cameroon, Lac region of Chad), and tend to gravitate towards each other more than their respective capitals. Many of these communities have historically experienced limited interactions with the state, reducing relationships to power centers." They went further to add that this "neglect has bred sentiments of marginalization and a disconnect from the state itself, resulting in limited overall ties."

In other words, the insurgency came as a result of the failure of the government to show its presence in some remote areas.

It is expedient to mention here that internally displaced persons taking refuge in various camps in the city of Maiduguri have now been moved back to their home towns: Konduga, Bama, Gwoza,Madagali just to mention but a few. Over 20,000 hostages were rescued through various commando-style raid and rescue missions by the Army. The Nigerian Army was also able to identify, monitor, and eliminate top Boko Haram commanders under General Buratai because of his ability to win the hearts and minds of the local population who saw in him the heart of sincerity and empathy. The people realized that the COAS was passionate about restoring peace and stability to Borno State and the entire North- East region of the country. Winning the hearts and minds of the local population was a major event that turned the table against the insurgents because it saw the emergence of a re-invigorated joint civil-military operations task force which is a joint task force composed of civil-military operations units from more than one Service. It provides support to the joint force commander in humanitarian or nation assistance operations, theatre campaigns, or a civil-military operation concurrent with or after regional conflict. It can organize military interaction among many governmental and governmental humanitarian agencies within the theatre. The Nigerian Army received international accolades from far and near between 2016 to late 2017. It was for this reason that the Brazilian Army and numerous organizations gave the COAS various awards.

The truth of the matter is that the insurgency happening in Nigeria is a very complex one and the Nigerian Army alone cannot quench it. It is only the political leadership that can tackle and solve the myriad challenges of endemic poverty, lack of opportunities, hate, bigotry, and corruption that is holding the Nigerian nation down. Without addressing these challenges, whatever gains Nigeria achieves under General Buratai will not last. Furthermore, if the Department of State Service (secret police), the police and the Immigration services can begin to live up to expectation by doing their job, the story of Boko Haram insurgency will have been entirely different. But in Nigeria we see a situation where other security agencies are missing in action; the Nigerian Army is the one leading the fight and doing the work of other security agencies.

One cardinal area where both the DSS, civil police and the NSA have underperformed is in the area of intelligence gathering and sharing. This is why the secret police is yet to identify a single financier of the insurgency even though most people in the northeast region believe that so many businessmen and politicians are supporting the insurgency for financial gains.

Nevertheless, there is a vocal school of thought that believes that General Buratai's leadership of the Army is nothing to write home about because the insurgents still carry out hit and run attacks on soft targets and soldiers get killed now and then. Such people failed to take into cognizance the fact that Nigeria used to be second in the World Terrorism Index from 2014 to 2015 but now the story has changed. This is to show that even the international community recognizes the fact that the security situation in Nigeria had improved under General Buratai. In 2014, "Nigeria experienced the largest increase in terrorist activity with 7,512 deaths in 2014, an increase of over 300% since 2013 and it also experienced the biggest year-on-year increase in deaths ever recorded with 5,662 more people being killed, and over 300 percent increase (WTI,2014). The most recent report of the Index showed that deaths as a result of Boko Haram insurgency have drastically reduced and Nigeria is now fourth on the Index.

To such people, I will say that they need to understand what is insurgency, its rationale and modus operandi, and of course its complexities and peculiarities. They will have to counterbalance this with the principles of human rights. According to the world-acclaimed scholar on terrorism, Philip H. Gordon who is a Senior Fellow for U.S. Foreign Policy at the Brookings Institution, "Victory in the war on terror will not mean the end of terrorism, the end of tyranny, or the end of evil, Utopian goals that have all been articulated at one time or another. Terrorism, after all (to say nothing of tyranny and evil), has been around for a long time and will never go away entirely. From the Zealots in the first century add to the Red Brigades, the Palestine Liberation Organization, the Irish Republican Army, the Tamil Tigers, and others in more recent times, terrorism has been a tactic used by the weak to produce political change. Like violent crime, deadly disease, and other scourges, it can be reduced and contained. But it cannot be eliminated." (Gordon,2007). This is a critical point because the goal of ending terrorism entirely is not only unrealistic but also counterproductive—just as is the pursuit of other Utopian goals.

Gordon went on to further explain in his book that victory in the war against terrorism, "means not the complete elimination of any possible terrorist threat— pursuing that goal will almost certainly lead to more terrorism, not less—but rather the reduction of the risk of terrorism to such a level that it does not significantly affect average citizens' daily lives, preoccupy their thoughts, or provoke an overreaction. At that point, even the terrorists will realize their violence is futile. Keeping this vision of victory in mind will not only avert considerable pain, expense, and trouble; it will also guide leaders toward the policies that will bring such a victory about (Gordon.2007).

If we consider the fact that great nations like the United States with all their military might and huge war chest can spend up to nineteen years fighting the Taliban in Afghanistan and yet couldn't achieve total victory, we will begin to appreciate the successes Nigeria, a developing nation can achieve under General Buratai without any external support in terms of troops.

America is no doubt winning the war in Afghanistan but she is not yet done with the Taliban. It is on record that a few officers and a handful of soldiers had died in the insurgency and my deepest condolences go to their respective families. I should like to point out the fact that many of those soldiers who died in the North-East died of terrorism attacks and not because they were overpowered by the insurgents. We must begin to understand that the insurgency, though closely linked to terrorism, is an entirely different phenomenon. The insurgents resort to terrorism because that is, in most instances the only means available to them to show their presence.

Before I conclude this essay, I want to list out some factors to show that the Nigerian military has won the war (but the government is yet to win the peace):

Foreign patrons or allies are cutting off support for Boko Haram insurgency;

There is massive support for the government and its security forces by a critical segment of the population;

Nigerians see the government as legitimate;

Sustained elimination of top commanders of the insurgency;

Internal conflict among the top commanders of the insurgency because of discouragement and a change of opinion;

The massive flight of commanders to safe havens because of fear of getting killed by the Army; Rapid decrease of insurgent forces;

Lack of any real territory and/or population to control by the insurgents;

The gradual strengthening of the economy which includes the recognition of Nigeria as the best in Africa;

Lack of any real evidence of the federal government's willingness to seek a negotiated settlement with the insurgents;

No any report of military plots, coup attempts, or massive desertion, defection, or surrender of security forces; and lastly, Lack of any exit strategy for Boko Haram leaders like Abubakar Shekau who doesn't have a plan or wherewithal to negotiate, surrender and transform his group into a political party or anything that can exist under a democratic setting.

At this juncture, I must point out that the COAS was able to achieve this great success through the input of gallant lieutenants.

In conclusion, Nigerians must have a rethink and begin to appreciate the efforts of the Nigerian Army and the relative peace we are enjoying in the country.

❖ ❖ ❖

APPENDIX C

❖ ❖ ❖

The lineage foundation of the two kingdoms (Biu and Mandaragirau) from the original Babur Kingdom can rightly be illustrated as shown below:

1. Yamtarawala - C. 1535-60 (Founder of Babur Kingdom)
2. Mari Virahyel
3. Dawi Dira Nala
4. Yamta Amba
5. Mai Yamta Kupaya Wadi
6. Mai Mari Watila Tampta
7. Mai Yamtara Banye 1680
8. Mai Mari Luku – 1690
9. Mai Jakwa Birtiktik – 1700
10. Mai Mari Thlama Bahara -1710

11. Mai Mari Tayar Wrinki 1720

12. Mai Dawi – 1730(Father of Mari Kopchi & Ali Sokar)

13. Mai Mari Kopchi and Mai Ali Sokar 1740 (Biu kingdom)

(Maidaragirau kingdom) WOVIRI CLAN DAGIL CLAN

LIST OF MANDARAGIRAU MAIS
(as shown by the colonial masters) Mai Ali Sokar (1) (brother to Mari Kopchi of Biu).

1. Mai Mari Bohilia (2) (Succeeded By His Son)
2. Mai Arri Kofali (3)
3. Mai Difuma (4)
4. Mai Dimanti (5)
5. Mai Mari Biya (6)
6. Mai Mari Manti (7)
7. Mai Arri (8)
8. Mai Mari (9) (Deposed In 1911)

❖ ❖ ❖

BIBLIOGRAPHY

❖ ❖ ❖

Adekunle, O. (2017) *Buratai Bags Brazilian Highest Military Award* . *Vanguard*. Available at: https://www. vanguardngr. com/2017/04/buratai-bags-brazilian-highest-military-honour/ (Accessed on 11 April 2019)

Agbese, P. (2016) *One Year and Buratai Shines Even More*. Legit. Com Available at: https://www. legit. ng/914076-one-year-read-achievements-chief-army-staff-tukur-buratai. html (Accessed on 20 July 2019)

Argys, L. M. , Rees, D. I. , Everett, S. L. , & Witoonchart, B. (2006). *Birth order and risky adolescent behaviour. Economic Inquiry, 44,* 215–233.

Antolini, D. (2009) *The Giant of Kandahar And The Lost Race Of The Nephilim*. Available at http:// www. thexplan. net/article/378/THE-GIANT-OF-KANDAHAR/it. (Accessed on 23March 2019)

Broome. F. (2016) What can you do to attract ghosts? *Ghosts 101*. Available at :https://ghosts101. com/ attract-ghosts/ (Accessed on May 11 2019)

Broome, F. (2008) *The haunting of John Alford Tyng*. Hollow Hill: The Ghost Haunting Website. Available at :https://hollowhill. com/haunting-john-alford-tyng/ (Accessed on 11May 2019)

Bamidele, S. *(2015) Counter Terrorist Trends and Analyses*. Vol. 7, No. 8 (September 2015), pp. 10-15

Bachman, J. G. , Wadsworth, K. N. , O'Malley, P. M. , Johnston, L. D. , & Schulenberg, J. E. (1997). *Smoking, drinking, and drug use in young adulthood: The impacts of new freedoms and new responsibilities*. Mahwah, NJ: Erlbaum.

Banks, L. (2006). The history of special operations psychological selection. In A. Mangelsdorff (Ed.), *Psychology in the service of national security* (pp. 83–95). Washington, DC: American Psychological Association.

Barrett, T. (2011). *The search for the forgotten thirty-four*. CreateSpace Independent Publishing Platform. Available at :https://www. createspace. com/3598732. (Accessed on 10 February 2019)

Bass, B. M. , & Riggio, R. E. (2006). *Transformational leadership (2nd ed.)*. Mahwah, NJ: Erlbaum.

Batson, C. D. (1991). *The altruism question: Toward a social–psychological answer*. Hillsdale, NJ: Erlbaum.

Becker, S. , & Eagly, A. (2004). The heroism of women and men. *American Psychologist, 59*, 163–178.

Black, L. (2015). *Are heroes born or made? An analysis of heroic behaviour based on U. S. military personnel and veterans*. (Unpublished doctoral dissertation). Pacific Graduate School of Psychology, Palo Alto University, Palo Alto, CA.

Bluglass, K. (2003). *Hidden from the holocaust: Stories of resilient children who survived and thrived*. Westport, CT: Praeger.

Bu, F. (2014). Sibling configurations, educational aspirations and attainment. Working paper series, 2014-11, Institute for Social and Economic Research, University of Essex. Retrieved from http://www. theguardian. com/society/2014/apr/26/firstborn-children-excel-study-reveals.

Balsamo. , Carpozi Jr. , (1997) *The Mafia: The Deadly Inside Story of Organised Crime*. W. H Great Britain: Allen and & Co Ltd Plc.

Collier, P. (2010) *War, Guns and Votes Democracy in Dangerous Places*. London: Bodley Vintage;245 Pages, Paperback.

Congressional Medal of Honour Society. (1994a). Master Sergeant Gordon, Gary, I, Medal of Honour citation. Available at: http://www. cmohs. org/ recipient-detail/2197/gordon-gary-i. php on 8/15/2013. (Accessed on 13 February 2018)

Congressional Medal of Honour Society. (1994b). Sergeant First Class, Shughart, Randall, D, Medal of Honour citation. Retrieved from: http://www. cmohs. org/recipient-detail/2198/shughart-randall-d. php on 8/15/2013. (Accessed on 13 February 2018)

Cougle, J. (2009). An examination of courageous behaviour in a laboratory setting. (Doctoral dissertation). Dissertation Abstracts International, 69.

Dalton, J. E. , Auchubon, I. N. , Tom, A. , Pederson, S. L. , & McFarland, R. E. (1993). MBTI profiles of Vietnam veterans with post-traumatic stress disorder. *Journal of Psychological Type*, 26, 3–8.

Emery, L. , Hess, T. , & Elliot, T. (2012). The illusion of the positive: The impact of natural and induced mood on older adults' false recall. *Aging, Neuropsychology, and Cognition*, 19, 677–698.

Fagin-Jones, S. , & Midlarsky, E. (2007). Courageous altruism: Personal and situational correlates of rescue during the Holocaust. *Journal of Positive Psychology*, 2, 136–147.

Fein, H. (1993). *Genocide: A sociological perspective*. London, UK: SAGE.

Fenwick, P. , & Brayne, S. (2011). End-of-life experiences: Reaching out for compassion, communication, and connection — Meaning of deathbed visions and coincidences. *American Journal of Hospice and Palliative Medicine*, 28(1), 7–15.

Franco, Z. E. , Blau, K. , & Zimbardo, P. G. (2011). Heroism: A conceptual analysis and differentiation between heroic action and altruism. *Review of General Psychology*, *15*, 99–113.

Gal, R. (1983). Courage under stress. In S. Breznitz (Ed.), *Stress in Israel* (pp. 65–91). New York, NY: Van Nostrand Reinhold.

Gal, R. (1995). Personality and intelligence in the military: The case of war heroes. In D. Saklofske, M. Zeidner (Eds.), *International Handbook of Personality and Intelligence* (pp. 727–737). New York, NY: Plenum.

Lt. T. Y General Buratai *(2017) I came in Ready to Make A Difference. Interview with General Buratai with Dr Abubakar M. S in Maiduguri for the North-east Star magazine. Vol. 4. No. 9. Abuja: Ellakkawi Bros. & Co Ltd.*

Global Terrorism Index (2015) *Measuring and Understanding the Impact of Terrorism*. World Relief Web . Available at :https://reliefweb. int/report/world/global-terrorism-index-2015-measuring-and-understanding-impact-terrorism. (Accessed on 20 July 2019)

Godden, M. (2017) The REAL reasons why some

people see ghosts, according to experts. Available at
:https://www. thesun. co. uk/news/4051536/reasons-why-people-see-ghosts-paranormal-activity-experts/
(Accessed on 15 April 2019)

Global Terrorism Index (2018). *World Relief Web.*
Available at https://reliefweb. int/report/world/global-terrorism-index-2018. (Accessed on 20 July 2019)

Gordon, P. H. (2008) *Winning the Right War:*
The Path to Security for America and the World.
Washington: Holt Paperbacks

Goldstein, R. (2006, January 7). Hugh Thompson,
62, who saved civilians at My Lai, dies. *New*
York Times. Retrieved from: http://www. nytimes.
com/2006/01/07/national/07thompson. html?_r=0.

Harrison, W. (2012). Beyond courage: The
psychology of heroism. (Unpublished doctoral
dissertation). Pacific Graduate School of Psychology,
Palo Alto University, Palo Alto, CA.

Hassan, R. (2008). Global rise of suicide terrorism:
An overview. *Asian Journal of Social Science*

Holmes, J. , & Marra, M. (2006). Humor and
leadership style. *International Journal of Humor*
Research

Hutchinson, J. , & Lema, J. (2009). Ordinary and
extraordinary narratives of heroism and resistance:
Uncovering resilience, competence and growth.
Counseling Psychology Review, *24*(3/4)

Jayawickreme, E. , & Di Stefano, P. (2012). How can we study heroism? Integrating persons, situ ations and communities. *Political Psychology*, *33*, 165–178.

Jobe, J. B. , Holgate, S. H. , & Sorapansky, T. A. (1983). Risk taking as motivation for volunteering for a hazardous experiment. *Journal of Personality*

Karni, G. , Solomon, Z. , Dekel, R. , & Neria, Y. (2003). Battlefield functioning and chronic PTSD: Associations with perceived self-efficacy and causal attribution. *Personality and Individual Differences*, *34*, 463–476.

Kinsella, E. L. , Ritchie, T. D. , & Igou, E. R. (2015). Zeroing in on heroes: A prototype analysis of hero features. *Journal of Personality and Social Psychology*

Kugel, U. (2015). Physical courage among military personnel and veterans (Order No. 3733316). Available from ProQuest Dissertations & Theses Global.

Levenson, M. R. (1990). Risk taking and personality. *Journal of Personality and Social Psychology*,

Miller, I. (2000). *The Mystery of Courage*. Cambridge, MA: Harvard University Press.

Monroe, K. R. (1994)."But what else could I do?" Choice, identity and a cognitive-perceptual theory of ethical political behaviour. *Political Psychology*

Myers, I. B. (1995). *Gifts differing: Understanding personality type* (2nd ed.). Palo Alto, CA: Consulting Psychologists Press.

Mohammed, A. , (2018) *The Legend of Buratai* Vol. 1. Lagos: Sprezzatura Publishing.

Mohammed, A. (2018) May 29: Nigeria's Democracy and Its Heroes. North-east Star magazine. Vol. 4. No. 8. Abuja: Ellakkawi Bros. & Co Ltd.

Omeni, A. (2017) *Counter-Insurgency in Nigeria: The Military and Operations against Boko Haram*, 2011-2017. Edition 1st Edition. London: Routledge.

Olaniyan, A. ((2018) *Once Upon a Game Reserve: Sambisa and the Tragedy of a Forested Landscape*. Arcadia Collection. Environment and Societal Portal. Available at :http://www. environmentandsociety. org/arcadia/once-upon-game-reserve-sambisa-and-tragedy-forested-landscape. (Accessed on 23 April 2019)

Powell, C. L. (1995) *My American Journey* New York: Random House.

Usman, B. (2015) A History of Biu. Abuja: Klamidas

www.ingramcontent.com/pod-product-compliance
Lightning Source LLC
Chambersburg PA
CBHW060839280326
41934CB00007B/844